WELCOME TO YOUR FINANCIAL LIFE

VIRGINIA B. MORRIS
KENNETH M. MORRIS

LIGHTBULB
PRESS ®

LIGHTBULB PRESS
Project Team

Design Director Dave Wilder
Design Kara W. Hatch
Design Assistants Mercedes Feliciano, Katharina Menner

Editors Mavis Morris, Tania Sanchez
Production and Illustration Antonina Colbert, Holly Duthie, Christopher Engel, Cadence Giersbach, Gary Lingard, James R. Lowenhaupt, Terry Marks, Mike Mulhern, Fanny Neira, Noah L. Rodriguez, Thomas F. Trojan, Edie Winograde

SPECIAL THANKS
Paul J. Benzon
Karen W. Lichtenberg, Starr Marcello

*D*oing something for the first time can be difficult and frustrating—learning to ride a bike, for example, or using a snowboard, or visiting a foreign country. But once you've gotten the basics down, your enjoyment far outweighs the trials of learning.

Getting a handle on your personal finances is really not much different, except perhaps that as your situation in life changes, there is always something new to learn. But what does hold true for making and managing your money is this: By understanding a few basic financial principles you can avoid the common pitfalls, help protect what you have, and make sound decisions about putting your money to work for you.

While personal finance and investing are not rocket science, things do get complicated. That's because there are often many choices available, and it's hard to know which is the right one for you. For example, are you better off making a large deposit and getting free checking or making no deposit and paying a fee for each check? Is it smarter to buy a car with a loan or lease the car instead? Which of the dozens of credit cards you're offered really is the best deal? And how should you invest the money in a retirement savings plan provided by your employer? (Are you kidding, why even think about retirement now!)

If you don't know the answers to these questions right off, don't panic. Most other people don't either. But that's one way to get ahead— knowing the important things to consider when making decisions about money. And that's really the reason we wrote this book—to share with you what we have experienced first hand, and what we have learned from others, especially our daughters as they started out and our wonderful, inquisitive staff at Lightbulb Press.

So the next time someone asks us, "Should I use the extra money I have to pay off my student loan or invest in stocks?" we can say, "Welcome to your financial life. And here's a little guide that will give you the answers to that and many other questions that can help ensure a bright financial future."

Virginia B. Morris   Kenneth M. Morris

WELCOME TO YOUR FINANCIAL LIFE

INTRODUCTION

AT THE BANK

FINANCE AT WORK

CREDIT AND DEBT

HOME FINANCE

FINANCIAL PLANNING

INVESTING

TAXES

A Financial Foundation

If you get off to a good start, you've got the framework for a secure future.

One of the things you discover as you start out on your own is that making decisions about money—especially managing your money—plays an increasingly larger part in your life.

Things that you may have taken for granted when you were in school or living at home—everything from where you sleep and what you eat to how to pay your credit card bills—suddenly require a lot more time and energy than they did before.

What you may also start to realize is how much you need to know to make smart financial decisions. While your common sense can get you through a lot, sooner or later you'll have to make choices you're not sure how to handle.

That's why this guide explores all of the important financial issues you'll face, from banking basics to picking a credit card, from reducing your current taxes to creating a long-term investment strategy.

DAY IN AND DAY OUT

Some of the financial questions that come up day-to-day can seem pretty minor. Should you be using a debit card or a credit card to buy your groceries? What's the best way to share living expenses with your roommate?

Other issues can be more perplexing: Should you pay off your student loans to wipe out your debt? Should you work freelance so you'll have time to pursue a project that's important to you?

On an even bigger scale, you may be wondering if it really makes sense to be putting money into a retirement savings plan when you expect to work another 40 years. And if you have a plan at work, should you also be putting money into an individual retirement account—an IRA?

BUMPS IN THE ROAD

It's easy to be overwhelmed by financial decisions, especially when they come at you all at once. Your parents may be so

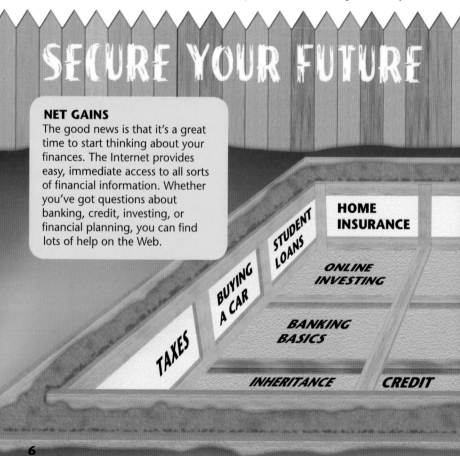

SECURE YOUR FUTURE

NET GAINS
The good news is that it's a great time to start thinking about your finances. The Internet provides easy, immediate access to all sorts of financial information. Whether you've got questions about banking, credit, investing, or financial planning, you can find lots of help on the Web.

STUDENT LOANS

HOME INSURANCE

ONLINE INVESTING

BUYING A CAR

BANKING BASICS

TAXES

INHERITANCE

CREDIT

happy that they don't have to do your taxes anymore that they dump files on your desk. And you may be baffled by the complexities of IRS Form W-4, which you have to fill out when you start each new job.

Similarly, if you're not sure what to do, you may pay more attention to convenience than cost, for example, in choosing a bank or a checking account. You may be tempted to buy a car you can't afford or sign up for telephone services you don't use. And it's entirely likely you'll be offered credit cards you don't need.

Without realizing what's at stake, you may postpone contributing to a 401(k) or other employer sponsored retirement plan because you don't think you can afford it. Or you may decide that since you've always been pretty healthy you can postpone paying for health insurance until your bank balance is in the black.

If even one of these situations is familiar to you, it's time to get some financial basics under your belt.

JUST THE BEGINNING

The frustrating thing about financial decisions is that you can't just make them and forget about them because each one has potential long-term con-sequences. That's why it's crucial to re-evaluate your situation periodically to make sure your earlier decisions are still the best ones. It's not too soon to set aside a day each year to examine every aspect of your financial life, decide what's working okay, and what you ought to change.

It's also smart to take a close look at your finances any time your life changes—if you move, for example, or change jobs, get married, have a child, or gain or lose a lot of money.

BY THE BOOK

In this book, you'll find a section on just about every financial subject you'll have to deal with.

You can start in the early chapters with the basics—like choosing bank accounts and evaluating job-related benefits—and go on to potentially more complex topics, like financial planning and investing. Or you can skip around, finding the information you need when you need it.

Throughout the book, you'll also find real-life stories from people like you who have been through some of the same financial situations you're facing. Check out what they have to say, and see what you can learn from their experiences.

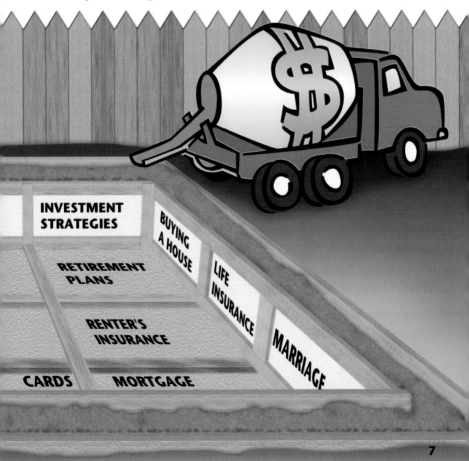

INVESTMENT STRATEGIES

BUYING A HOUSE

RETIREMENT PLANS

LIFE INSURANCE

RENTER'S INSURANCE

MARRIAGE

CARDS   MORTGAGE

Banking Basics

It's hard to get by without a bank account.

When you think about life's necessities, finding a bank probably isn't at the top of your list. In fact, the idea of putting a bank in the same category as having a place to live and enough to eat may seem downright bizarre. But unless you're paid in cash, pay all your bills in person, and aren't trying to save for the future, it's hard to think how you could get along without a bank or its not-for-profit equivalent, the credit union.

The catch is that if you've seen one bank, you haven't necessarily seen them all. The services you can get, and what those services will cost you, vary significantly from bank to bank. So does the way you're treated if you've got questions or problems.

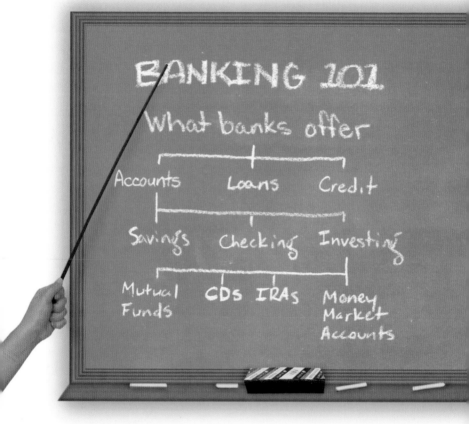

THE BIG PICTURE

Banks are essential to making the economy work. They make loans, which you can use to pay college expenses, buy a car, or purchase a home. They issue credit cards, which let you buy products or services when you need or want them and pay for them over time. And banks provide financial services such as checking, savings, and investment accounts.

The money you deposit in your checking and savings accounts is an important source of funds that the bank uses to make loans. And the interest you pay on your loans pays for the interest you earn on your savings.

But banks don't fill the role of finan-cial intermediary just because it's good for you, or for the economy. They want to make a profit. To do that, they charge you more to borrow than they pay you for keeping money in the bank. In fact, they rarely pay you anything for the money you have in your checking account—which you can withdraw at any time—and very little on regular savings accounts, which give you similar access.

And they charge fees on most of these accounts to help cover the costs of processing checks, providing account statements, tellers, ATMs, and multiple branches, plus the costs of advertising and promotion to attract your business.

YOU CAN BANK ON IT

You may have some uncertainties where money is concerned, like whether you'll be able to live on what you earn and whether you'll be more financially secure in the future than you are today. Banks can't solve those problems, but putting your money in a bank will provide one safety net in an otherwise uncertain world. Banks promise that up to $100,000 of your money, deposited in one or more of their accounts, is safe.

Here's the story: The **Federal Deposit Insurance Corporation (FDIC)**, a government agency, insures accounts in its member banks, which include most banks in the US. (There's separate, comparable insurance for credit unions.)

The $100,000 limit—which some have suggested should be increased to reflect the impact of inflation—applies per depositor per bank. For example, if you had $100,000 in a **certificate of deposit (CD)** in one bank and another $100,000 in a CD in another bank, both accounts would be covered. But if you had $200,000 in one CD, only half would be insured.

You can actually qualify for more than the $100,000 coverage at a single bank if your assets are in different types of accounts. For example, an **individual retirement account (IRA)** is insured separately from a taxable account. So is a trust account. And you qualify for up to $50,000 coverage on an account you own jointly with someone else.

What's not insured is any money you invest through a bank that's not in a checking or savings account. For example, money in a mutual fund the bank sells is not insured, even if the name of the fund includes the name of the bank. But money in the bank's money market account is insured. The bank is required to tell you which accounts are insured and which are not. Be sure you know which are which.

HABITUAL BEHAVIOR

Finding a bank that will best meet your needs depends, in large part, on your spending and saving habits—or the ones you're trying to cultivate. The more you know about how you're likely to use your account, the more effective your search can be. To get started, ask yourself these questions:

- How many checks do you typically write each month, and how often do you withdraw cash at the ATM?
- Do you have enough cash available to meet a minimum balance requirement for a no-cost or interest-bearing checking account, and will you be able to keep that amount in your account?
- Do you have time to get to the bank during banking hours, or do you need a bank that's open nights and weekends?
- Would you like the option of banking online or over the phone?

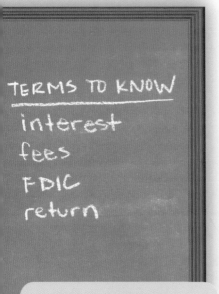

TERMS TO KNOW
interest
fees
FDIC
return

IN CASE OF EMERGENCY

Most financial advisers suggest creating an **emergency fund** with three to six months' worth of income. That way you'll have some backup if you face a major financial emergency, such as getting sick or being laid off.

Ideally, an emergency fund should be fairly **liquid**, which means the money is available as cash or can be converted to cash easily with little or no loss of value. But the fund should also produce some **return**, or increase in value. Certificates of deposit (CDs) and money market accounts will probably fit these needs.

The goal of having your money make some money is one reason your emergency fund probably shouldn't be in a checking account. The other reason is that it's too easy to spend.

Shopping for a Bank

Finding a bank is like choosing a pair of shoes:
You want the right style and size at the right price.

Before you settle on a place to bank, it's smart to know what your options are. There are more choices than you might think.

Among the things that can help you decide are the range of services you need, how convenient it will be to manage your money day-to-day, and whether you're getting a good financial deal.

As important as your decision is, though, you're not making a lifetime commitment. If you're not happy with the level of service a bank provides or if you think the fees are too high, you can always close your account and take your money someplace else. Making a switch is easy, and there's no charge.

THE BIG PLAYERS

If you live in or near a large city, your choices may include one or more large **national** or **regional banks** whose names are recognized around the world.

These institutions serve individuals and businesses at hundreds, and sometimes thousands, of branches. In addition to a variety of checking and savings accounts, they typically offer extensive investment services, a full range of loans, multiple ATM locations, online banking, and automatic bill payment.

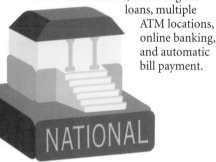

SHOP AROUND
If you do a little research, you may be able to find a bank that offers special deals to new customers or to the new employees of their corporate and not-for-profit clients. It can pay to ask around. And you can get help finding a credit union by calling the **Credit Union National Association (CUNA)** at 800-356-9655, or going to www.cuna.org.

TWO FOR ONE
You might consider using two banks—one online and one local. That way you get the advantage of 24-hour access and reduced fees while keeping enough cash in a local bank for ATM withdrawals. If you're having your paycheck directly deposited, you can split the deposit between the two in whatever proportion works for you. And if you need a bank check or a signature guarantee, the local bank can provide it.

But convenience has a price tag. Charges for basic and special services are often higher than you might pay at local banks or credit unions. And you may need a minimum balance of several thousand dollars to get free checking and ATM use, a reduced rate on credit cards or loans, or the best interest rate on your savings account.

KEEP IT LOCAL
If you're looking for more personal service at a better price, you might want to check out **community banks**. They offer checking and savings accounts, the standard array of loans, and sometimes full-scale investment and online services.

Local banks are more likely to have weekend and evening hours than national or regional banks. Plus, their minimum balance requirements for free checking and ATM use tend to be lower, and their fees and other charges may be lower as well.

But there can be limitations. Local banks typically have just a few branches. If there isn't one near your home or office, it can be inconvenient to handle transactions you have to do in person or get cash without paying to use another bank's ATM.

CREDIT UNIONS

If you have the opportunity, you might consider joining a **credit union**—a cooperative, not-for-profit financial institution created by a company, labor union, community group, or other organization. Each credit union sets its own eligibility requirements, which you have to meet if you want to join. For example, you may have to work for a company to be eligible for its credit union.

Credit union fees and loan rates are usually lower, and the interest rates they pay are usually higher than their for-profit competition, making them the most economical place to bank. And they have a reputation for being more friendly.

The potential limitation is the range of services. While larger credit unions offer most, if not all, of the accounts and services you need, smaller ones may have limited choices. And many credit unions have just one office and are open only limited hours.

NON-BANK BANKS

You can also do your banking with banks established by brokerage firms, insurance companies, mutual fund companies, and other financial institutions. Some of them are **non-bank banks**, which offer only deposit services—that is, checking and savings accounts but not loans. Others offer everything a traditional bank offers, and then some: a variety of checking and savings accounts, ATM and debit cards, electronic bill paying, online account access, and more.

If you're already doing business with a financial services company, one-stop money management can be extremely convenient. And you may get better rates and pay lower fees than at other banks.

But there are some potential drawbacks. You may need to have a fairly large minimum balance, and since most non-bank banks don't own their own ATMs, you may end up paying cash withdrawal fees to use other machines. However, some non-bank banks refund those fees up to a monthly limit of $6 to $10.

VIRTUAL BANKS

The newest banks are **virtual banks**, which exist only online and have no bricks-and-mortar branches. Some are full-service, while others offer savings and investment products plus mortgage loans but not checking accounts. Virtual banks typically charge lower fees and pay higher interest because of low overhead. And you can check your transactions in real time, as they happen, rather than at the end of the banking day or the end of the month.

Like non-bank banks, virtual banks don't have branches or own ATM machines, so you'll have to make deposits electronically or by mail, and pay ATM fees for using other banks' machines. To cover that expense, some online banks reimburse you for a certain number of ATM withdrawals each month.

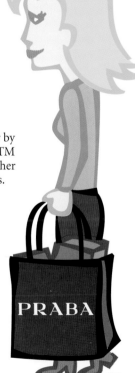

Online Banking

Banking—like almost everything else—has moved onto the Web.

More and more people are banking online, and with good reason. In addition to the 24/7/365 convenience of not having to leave your home (or office) to check your balance, you can move money from one account to another, pay your bills, invest, and borrow through one online account. About the only thing you can't do is get your computer to give you cash—though that day may come.

SOFTWARE USERS

SAVE MONEY
SAVE TIME
IT'S CONVENIENT

GETTING CONNECTED

Whether you use online services offered by a bricks-and-mortar institution or put your money in a **virtual bank** that exists only online, there are two ways to access your account.

You can buy special banking software, like Microsoft® Money or Quicken®, so you can connect to your bank to authorize transactions. Offline, these programs let you handle all kinds of financial planning and recordkeeping.

Or, you can connect directly to your account through the bank's website without having to buy and install special software. Many people find that connecting directly has big advantages:

- You can get to your account from any computer, since you don't have to install any software
- You're connecting directly to your bank's secure network
- It may be cheaper, as some banks charge a monthly fee if you connect through a third party, plus you don't have the cost of the software

PAY YOUR BILLS

Electronic bill payment is one of the most popular features of online banking. You can have your bank pay certain bills automatically each month just by providing the payment information the bank needs and identifying the account to debit. Some banks pay these bills as they're due, rather than when they arrive. Others let you set the day on which a specific bill, such as your car lease, will be paid.

If you prefer to authorize bill payments yourself, you can do that too. You access your account once or twice a month, key in the amounts you want to pay to a list of established payees or one you're adding,

BANKS PROVIDE DATA

Using an online-only bank has been a great way to reduce fees and get easy access to all of my finances from anywhere. The only downside is that, without a branch to go to, I have to set up direct deposit for my paycheck and mail in any other deposits.
—Tim W., 22

and indicate when you want each payment made. The bank handles the rest. The payments may be made electronically to some payees and by check to others, depending on arrangements the bank makes.

Some banks handle electronic bill payment for free, while others charge a small fee, usually less than $10 a month.

NET SAFETY

Some people worry that online transactions aren't as safe as the ones you make in the traditional way, with cash or paper checks. But banks take lots of precautions to protect you and themselves from fraud or theft. And you have the same legal protections with online accounts as you do with conventional accounts.

Bank records are insulated by a **firewall**, a computer that controls the flow of information between the bank's internal computer system and the outside world. A firewall is designed to ensure that your personal data, and all the information the bank keeps, can't be stolen or manipulated by outsiders.

Banks also provide **data encryption**. When you communicate with the bank's site, your passwords, personal data, and other secure information are scrambled, or encrypted, by the site. No one who doesn't have the key to unscramble the data can tap into your account.

You use a **personal identification number**, or **PIN**, to identify yourself whenever you enter the bank's site. It may be the same PIN that you use for your ATM or debit card, but it's probably a good idea to choose a different one. That way, even if one PIN is compromised, the other isn't.

In addition to those safeguards, many online banks automatically log you off if you're idle for more than a few minutes, so no one can get into your account if you walk away from your desk. And some banks send you e-mail alerts if someone has tried to get into your account with an incorrect password.

NET GAINS

If you're wondering if online banking will work for you, here's what some fans say about it.

It's convenient. You can check on your balance in real time at any time, so you always know how much money you have.

It saves time. If you hate standing in line, or if it's hard for you to get to your bank during banking hours, then doing your banking online can be a lifesaver.

It may save you money. The fees are often cheaper and the interest you earn is higher at virtual banks than anywhere but credit unions. And you do save on postage.

ENTER YOUR PIN XXXX

IS ELECTRONIC PAYMENT SMART?

If electronic bill payment appeals to you, you can set it up for as many or as few payees as you like. Some people prefer to pay only predictable bills this way—like rent or mortgage, local telephone, or Internet access. They'd rather pay bills that can vary a lot from month to month—such as credit card charges—themselves. That way, you decide how much or how little of a bill to pay.

Check It Out

Checking accounts take center stage in your day-to-day finances, and you can open one of several styles.

To pay your rent, cover your credit card, cable, and utility bills, buy your groceries, and repay your student loans, you almost certainly need a **checking account**. It's the only way to authorize the transfer of funds, whether you do it in writing or handle everything electronically.

Choosing the checking account that's best for you can be complicated, since accounts come in several varieties. Just look over the product offerings in a couple of banks or scroll through a few bank websites to get a sense of what's available.

IN THE BANK

A **regular checking account** with a conventional or online bank is likely to cost you—unless you can find a way to avoid it. Most banks charge either a monthly fee, a fee for each check or ATM withdrawal, or sometimes a combination of monthly and per-use fees. Charges can range upward from 35 cents per check and $1 per ATM withdrawal, and flat fees run, on average, from $7.50 to $15 a month.

Some banks may offer free checking and ATM use for a short time to attract your business. And most banks waive their fees if you keep a minimum balance in your checking account or in a combination of accounts in the bank. The catch here is the minimum can seem pretty maximum, though amounts vary. You may also qualify for free checking if your paycheck is deposited directly into your account.

Ask about all the possible combinations to quality. You can usually count the money in an interest-paying or investment account towards your minimum. Some banks also count your mortgage or other loan balance toward the minimum.

A SCALE OF FRILLS

Some banks offer a scaled-down version of their regular checking account, called **no-frills** or **basic checking**. If you write only a few checks a month and you don't withdraw money very often, it's something to consider. But for many working people, it's too restrictive—and the fees can be steep if you go over the limits.

At the other end of the scale, some banks offer combined accounts, called **relationship accounts**, that provide everything but the proverbial kitchen

BASIC

WORD CHECK

Checking accounts are actually transaction accounts. That means you can authorize the bank to transfer money from your account to another person or organization either by writing a check that includes the word "Pay to the order of" or by electronic transfer. In contrast, a savings account is a non-transaction account and the only things you can do are withdrawals or transfers—electronic or traditional—to another account in your name.

sink: no-fee credit cards, loan discounts, and the like. If the required minimum balance for this kind of account gets you free checking, there's probably nothing to lose, provided you need enough of the features the account offers.

INTEREST BEARING

CREDIT UNION

REGULAR

CHECKING, CREDIT UNION STYLE

If you're banking at a **credit union**—which might sound like a contradiction, but there's not really any other way to say it—you handle transactions in the same way you do at a bank. But instead of writing checks, you write what are known as **share drafts**.

The big difference is in the cost. Most credit unions don't impose fees for checking beyond the modest annual fee for membership, which is sometimes as little as $25. And if they require minimum deposits at all, it's much more likely to be hundreds rather than thousands of dollars.

DOING DOUBLE DUTY

One way to manage a minimum balance requirement is to put the money you've set aside for your emergency fund in a bank CD or money market account.

The money is safe, which meets one of the basic criteria for an emergency fund. And if you're ever in serious enough financial trouble to withdraw the money, the potential lost interest or below-minimum fees will probably be the least of your worries.

WEIGHING IN

If you have to maintain a minimum balance to get free checking, you might want to ask yourself a few questions:
- How many checks are you going to write, and how many times will you use the ATM?
- Would you make out better, financially speaking, by investing the minimum elsewhere and paying the fees for a basic, no-frills account?
- Should you investigate other banks, credit unions, virtual banks, or non-bank banks where you could get the same service and convenience at a lower cost?

A NEW INTEREST IN CHECKING

Like regular checking, an **interest-bearing checking account** lets you write as many checks as you want each month and use the bank's ATMs. The added benefit of these accounts is that you earn interest on your balance at the rate the bank sets, often about the same as you'd earn on a savings account.

So why wouldn't you choose to earn while you spend? Well, unless you maintain the minimum balance—an amount the bank determines—you not only forfeit the interest but typically owe more—sometimes much more—in fees than you would for a regular account at the same bank. Those fees can kick in for any month your balance drops below the minimum, sometimes even if it's just for a day or two or just a few dollars.

In most cases, even one month of unexpected fees can outweigh what you could earn in interest over several months. So as great as interest-bearing accounts may sound, you'll want to figure out if you can earn as much some other way, without the pressure.

15

Debit Cards

If debit cards are the future of banking, is cash history?

As the pennies pile up in your kitchen drawer, or you search for one more quarter so you can finally do the laundry, you may feel like all the talk about moving toward a cashless society is completely unrealistic. But think again. How often do you pay with plastic of one kind or another?

In the age of direct deposit and electronic bill payment, you're probably handling lots of financial transactions by swiping, dipping, or waving a card at a machine that can read it. Sometimes the card in question is a credit card, but it's more and more likely to be a **debit card**.

IT STARTED WITH THE ATM

Believe it or not, the first bank card—more commonly known as an **ATM card**—was introduced back in 1969. But until cards became common in the 1970s, the only ways to get cash were to stand in line at your bank or find someplace that would cash a check for you.

As it turns out, cash withdrawals were only the tip of the ATM iceberg. You can handle almost all your banking business with an ATM card, from transferring money to paying your credit card bill. And you can use your ATM card, or its newer sibling, the debit card—sometimes called a **cash plus card**—to make **point-of-sale (POS)** purchases by swiping it through the same type of machine you use to make credit card purchases.

SPLIT PERSONALITIES

To make a purchase with a plain ATM card, you type in your **personal identification number (PIN)** just as you do to withdraw cash. You don't have to sign anything, though you do get a receipt for your records.

You can use debit cards the same way—and other ways. That's where things can get a little murky. Sometimes you have to authorize a debit card transaction with your PIN, but sometimes you don't. When you don't use a PIN, you sign a receipt just as you would if you were charging the purchase to your credit card.

Some debit cards go one step further: They can work either as debit or credit

cards. If you're using the card as a debit card, you may either enter your PIN or sign a receipt, depending on where you're shopping. And if you're using the card as a credit card, you never enter the PIN, but you usually do have to sign.

Confused yet?

HOW DEBIT CARDS WORK

When you use an ATM or debit card, the amount of your purchase is **debited**, or subtracted, from your account and transferred electronically to the seller's account. There are usually no limits on the number of transactions you can make in the course of a day, though most banks set a daily dollar limit.

The amount you can spend per day is often the same amount that you can withdraw as cash, though they're counted separately. For example, if your withdrawal limit is $500 a day, your debit limit may also be $500. That means you could deplete your account by $1,000 a day—if you had that much money available. At other banks, one daily limit applies to both withdrawals and purchases.

If you have overdraft protection, you can debit up to the limit of your overdraft line of credit. But remember, you owe interest on the amount that the bank transfers to your checking account to cover your debt.

THE POPULARITY POLL

Banks love debit cards. It's much less expensive to process electronic debits than it is to process checks. And banks collect fees from retailers based on

the amount of your debit purchases, just as they do when you use a credit card.

Retailers like debit cards despite the fees they may have to pay—typically a percentage of the transaction—since people tend to buy more when it's easy to pay. And retailers do have the right to add a transaction fee to your bill if they choose. Further, debit cards reduce or eliminate the need to accept checks, which may be harder to get approved than cards and always carry the risk that they may bounce or that payment may be stopped.

So where does that leave you? There's no question that debit cards are handy. You don't need cash to go to the grocery store, and you can usually get $20 or more in cash on top of the amount of the sale. That eliminates a trip to an ATM and may save you $1.50 or more in fees. And being able to use a single card for debit or credit can also make your life easier.

Another plus is that using a debit card can help you keep your finances under control.

But even if you don't charge totally beyond your means the way you might with credit, a debit card still makes it possible to spend more than you have in your account. And if you end up overdrafting, you'll owe interest that can be even higher than you'd pay on a credit card.

Protected Plastic

The law is on your side if your debit card ends up in the wrong hands.

One reason you may be so comfortable using plastic is that you don't have to carry cash. But what happens if you lose your debit card or it's stolen?

PROTECTING YOUR MONEY

The danger is that if someone uses your debit card without your permission, they can withdraw your entire balance, plus the full amount of your overdraft line of credit.

But all is not lost. You can get back almost everything that's taken from your account—if you act reasonably quickly.

That's because all **electronic fund transfers**, or **EFTs**, are governed by the **Federal Reserve Board's Regulation E (Reg E)**, which spells out in specific detail what your rights are and how they must be protected. The bottom line is that if you notify your bank that your card is missing, or that money you didn't take is gone from your account, within the time frame Reg E specifies, the money must be restored to your account.

THE TICKING CLOCK

Reg E spells out two lines of defense for protecting your account from electronic theft.

If you report a lost or stolen card within two days of discovering that it's gone, the most you can end up losing is $50, no matter how much is missing from your account. In fact, in some cases, you may not lose any money at all, even if someone uses your card.

Remember, too, that Reg E doesn't require that the report be within two days of the actual loss, since it's possible you may not discover it's gone right away.

If you don't realize your card is gone until you get a bank statement

reporting withdrawals or purchases you didn't make, you still have 60 days from the postmark on the statement to report the loss or misuse. As long as you're within that time limit, you still won't lose more than $50.

But if you miss the 60-day deadline, you could lose all the money that's taken from your account after the 60-day period ends—provided there's anything left—plus up to $500 of what was taken during the 60-day period.

Banks have the right to make sure you're not trying to rip them off. Despite their potential losses, they have the burden of proving that they could have stopped someone from using your card if you'd notified them promptly. Even if they win, the most you can lose is $500.

your report or believes the evidence doesn't support your claims, getting a loss resolved can be time-consuming and potentially expensive.

SAFETY PINS

Sooner or later you're likely to lose a debit card or have it stolen.

As long as your **PIN** isn't written on the card or some other obvious place, it'll be pretty tough for a thief to get far at an ATM or with a card reader. Some ATM machines even swallow a card if someone has typed in three incorrect PINs in a row.

Protecting a debit card that can be activated with a signature is harder, since retailers don't always check closely. But be sure to sign the back anyway. That way there's always a chance someone will discover the forgery and refuse the sale.

DEBITING A LEMON
The one situation where you're not covered with a debit card is if you buy defective merchandise. While most credit cards don't make you pay for purchases of poor quality, if you buy a piece of junk with a debit card, the money you spent is gone as far as the bank is concerned.

THE HASSLES
The bigger issue with a stolen card, of course, is the hassle. If someone has used your card before you realize it's gone, your account could be bled dry. That may mean bounced checks, angry creditors, late fees, and a host of other problems.

Your bank initially has ten days to investigate your report and refund any money that it agrees was withdrawn without your permission—potentially minus $50. If it wishes, the bank can extend its investigation for up to 45 days. But if you've filed a written report, it must put the disputed amount back into your account within ten business days so you won't be left high and dry.

The bank has more flexibility with accounts open less than 30 days. It can take 20 days to finish an initial inquiry and refund your money, and up to 90 days for an extended investigation.

Debit card problems are typically resolved quickly. But if the bank questions

THE WRITTEN WORD
Whether you report a lost card within two days or 60, your bank can ask for a written report of your loss within ten business days. Do it. And do it on time.

In fact, it's always smart to write a letter about any dispute that involves money and save a copy for your files.

Finding Inner Balance

Keeping good records is crucial to achieving harmony in your financial life.

If you keep track of the checks you write, the cash you withdraw, and any electronic transfers you authorize, the account balance that pops up on an ATM screen or appears on your bank statement shouldn't take you by surprise. But if you don't stay on top of your account, your records and the bank's are likely to be out of sync.

That can be an inconvenience—or worse. So until the day comes when there are no more hand-written checks and no more cash transactions, you'll probably have to resign yourself to balancing your checking account on a regular basis.

That means being sure that the amount the bank thinks you have in your account is fairly close to what you think you have, and that there are no debits you didn't authorize.

YOUR LEDGER IS YOUR FRIEND

When you open a checking account, you get a **ledger** to keep track of your cash flow. Ledgers come in different shapes and sizes, and you may find that one type works better for you than the others.

With a **carbon-copy ledger**, you automatically create a copy of any check you write. But you don't have a place to record electronic transfers or ATM withdrawals, and there's no place to add deposits or credits or subtract the current check from your balance.

Some ledgers are **check stubs** that start life attached to checks but are left behind as the checks are used. There's a place on the stub to write the amount of the check and to whom it was written. And there may be a section you can use to update the current balance, though you have to transfer the numbers from the previous stub.

The most common record-keeper is a **separate ledger**, which fits into the top of your checkbook. Each time you write a check, deposit money, or make an ATM withdrawal, the idea is to write the date and the amount in the ledger. It's set up to make adding or subtracting each transaction easy, so you can keep a running record of your balance.

FINDING TRUE BALANCE

When your bank mails you a monthly statement, or when you check your statement online, you can compare the amount the bank says you have with what your records show. Figuring out how to make them match if there's a big discrepancy isn't a lot of fun. But it'll help you stay in control, financially speaking.

The worksheet on the back of your monthly statement walks you through the process. But be prepared to ask yourself these questions:

- Have all the checks you've written cleared your account and been subtracted on the bank statement? (If they haven't, you'll need to subtract those amounts from the bank's figures to get your real balance.)
- Have you subtracted all your electronic debits, including any fees, in your records?
- Have you added in all your deposits and credits, including direct deposits and interest if it applies?
- Have you added and subtracted entries correctly?

GET OVERDRAFT PROTECTION

If you miscalculate and **overdraw**, or write checks for more money than you actually have in your account, you could be hit with a substantial fee from your bank and potentially another one from the bank of the person you paid. You can avoid those charges, and potential embarrassment, if you arrange for **overdraft protection**. With it, the bank will transfer enough money to your account to cover the check.

Though the transfer is actually a loan that you'll have to repay with interest, there's no charge if you don't use the protection. Think of it as wearing suspenders as well as a belt. Just make sure you don't use it too often, or the interest you rack up could catch you with your pants down.

DOING THE MATH

Ending balance
  on your statement
− Any outstanding
  checks
―――――――――
= Balance in your ledger
+ Any unrecorded credits
− Any unrecorded fees

- Have you accidentally transposed numbers, entering $85.85 for $58.58? (It's a more common error than you might think!)

BANKS MAKE MISTAKES, TOO

Although banks don't usually make errors in addition or subtraction, they're not perfect. Tellers can transpose the amount of a deposit, and other information can be entered incorrectly. So keep all your deposit slips, ATM and debit card receipts, and other slips of paper until you've checked them against your monthly statement.

If you find what you think is an error in your statement, question it. And be sure to write a letter, as well as make a phone call, since you may need to prove that you made an inquiry if the problem isn't resolved quickly.

HELPFUL HINTS

There are ways to keep things under control:

Use technology. Electronic records are more current than printed statements. You can check your balance and recent transactions on your bank's ATM (though you'll want to be sure there's not a fee for getting the information when you're not authorizing a transaction). You can use a toll-free **voice response system (VRS)** if your bank offers one. And online banks update your records either in real time or at the end of the business day.

Limit your ATM and debit card transactions. If you hit the ATM every two or three days, or use your debit card for lots of small purchases, you may want to rethink your habits if you're having trouble keeping track of what you spend. But you do have to weigh fewer transactions against the convenience (and safety) of not having to carry cash.

Check your statement when it arrives. Your bank must respond to your questions about potential errors, but it has the right to require that inquiries occur promptly. In some cases you have up to 60 days from the date you get your statement, but in other cases it's just 14 days. The bank must give you information outlining these policies—make sure you're aware of them.

The Savings Route

Opening a savings account can help pave the way to financial security.

If you're building an emergency fund, saving for a big purchase, or getting money together to invest, using an insured savings account can put you on the right road. Most banks offer a variety of savings accounts. So do credit unions.

In addition to these basic savings accounts, other popular bank savings options are **money market accounts**, which combine savings with limited check-writing privileges, and **certificates of deposit (CDs)**.

GETTING INTERESTED

With a savings account, you make money on the money in your account by earning **interest**, or a percentage of your balance, at a specific rate on a regular schedule. What you earn depends on the interest rate the bank pays—typically about the same rate that other banks are paying on similar accounts. That rate, in turn, depends on the rate that banks are earning on the loans they make and on what it costs the banks to borrow from each other.

REGULAR RULES

The most basic accounts, where you can deposit and withdraw money at any time, are called **regular savings**, or sometimes **statement savings accounts**. What that means is that any activity in the account—deposits, withdrawals, fees, or interest earnings—and your current balance are reported in a printed or online account statement, usually once a month.

You earn interest on a regular savings account only if you keep at least the required minimum on deposit. If your balance is lower, some banks don't pay interest and others may charge a fee for holding your money. Unless you qualify for exemption from the fee—by being a full-time student or older than 65—you're stuck. The alternative is to look for an account without a required minimum or wait until you have the $500 or whatever is required.

In reality, though, you don't put money in a regular account for the earnings. Whatever the interest rate is, it's likely to be the lowest one the bank offers. You just want to avoid having to pay to keep your money on deposit.

MONEY MARKET ACCOUNTS

Most banks offer hybrid accounts—part checking, part saving—called **money market accounts (MMAs)** or sometimes **money market deposit accounts**. They're comparable to money market mutual funds, but have the advantage of FDIC insurance.

MMAs typically pay higher interest rates than regular savings accounts, and may offer **blended** or **tiered** rates, which means you can earn an even

higher rate on large balances or on part of your balance over a certain level.

And you can usually make a limited number of cash transfers or write a limited number of checks—often a total of three—against your account each month.

The catch is that there are substantial service fees if your account falls below the bank's minimum required balance. You may also forfeit your interest if the balance drops below the minimum, or you may face both penalties.

LUXURY MODELS

Certificates of deposit (CDs)—called **share certificates** at a credit union—are high-end savings accounts. They generally pay interest at a higher rate than other bank or credit union accounts, so it should come as no surprise that there are some strings attached.

What makes CDs different from regular savings accounts is that they're **time deposits**. That means that when you open a CD you agree to commit your money for a specific **term**, or period of time. You also agree that if you withdraw money from the CD before it **matures** when the term ends, you'll forfeit some or all of the interest you would have earned.

Typical terms include six months, a year, two and a half years, and five years. But the term may be any period you and the bank agree on. The longer the term, the slightly higher the interest you're likely to earn. There may be a minimum deposit—often $500—and some banks may pay slightly higher rates for large deposits.

When a CD matures, you can roll over the money into another CD, transfer your money to a different account, or have the bank send you a check. But you must tell the bank what you want it to do by the deadline it sets, or the decision will be made for you. When the bank decides, your CD is usually renewed for the same term as the expiring one at the bank's current rate for a CD of that length and principal.

ISN'T IT INTERESTING?

When banks advertise the interest rates on their savings accounts, they tell you the **nominal rate** and the **annual percentage yield (APY)**. The nominal, or named rate, is the rate they pay. The APY is what you earn over the course of a year, expressed as a percentage of your principal.

What you actually earn depends on whether the account pays **simple** or **compound interest**. Simple interest is calculated annually on the amount you deposit. With compound interest, which can be paid daily, monthly, or quarterly, the interest is added to your principal to form a new base on which you earn the next round of interest.

How can you tell whether interest is simple or compound? If the nominal rate and the APY are the same, you're earning simple interest. If the APY is higher, the interest is compound.

GONE BUT NOT FORGOTTEN
Most banks have phased out **passbook savings accounts**, which you may remember fondly or not—depending on how often you lost your passbook.

With these accounts, you handed the teller your passbook each time you made a deposit or withdrawal. The teller would run the book through a machine that calculated any interest due, enter the current transaction, and calculate your new balance.

Nuts and Bolts

There's a lot more to banking than writing an occasional check.

To get your banking experience off to a good start, it's smart to be able to talk the bank's language.

Available funds is the money in your account that you have the right to withdraw or transfer. Cash you deposit is available immediately, as are electronic transfers. Checks become available following the clearing guidelines established by the Federal Reserve. Mutual fund money market accounts with check-writing privileges set their own schedule for when deposits are available.

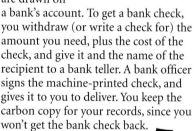

Bank checks, sometimes called cashier's checks, are drawn on a bank's account. To get a bank check, you withdraw (or write a check for) the amount you need, plus the cost of the check, and give it and the name of the recipient to a bank teller. A bank officer signs the machine-printed check, and gives it to you to deliver. You keep the carbon copy for your records, since you won't get the bank check back.

A **bounced check** is a check that you've written but that your bank refuses to pay either because there isn't enough money in your account to cover it or the funds you put in to cover it aren't available yet. If a check bounces, the bank typically charges you a fee, sometimes as much as $35 or more. One solution is to arrange for overdraft privileges, a line of credit the bank taps on your behalf to cover your checks.

A **cancelled check** is a check your bank has paid. The place and date when the check was deposited are printed on the back. Cancelled checks are proof of payment, but you are more likely to receive an electronic or photocopy rather than the check itself back.

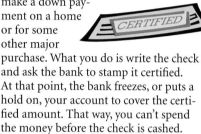

Certified checks are personal checks that your bank guarantees it will honor. You might need one to make a down payment on a home or for some other major purchase. What you do is write the check and ask the bank to stamp it certified. At that point, the bank freezes, or puts a hold on, your account to cover the certified amount. That way, you can't spend the money before the check is cashed.

Float is the time lag between when you write a check and when your bank debits your account. If you write a check before you have funds available to cover it, and it clears faster than you expect, your check may bounce. When you make an ATM withdrawal or use a debit card, there is no float.

WHEN CAN YOU WITHDRAW?

How fast money deposited in your account is available to you depends on several factors, including the type of check, where the bank it's written

Type of check
Federal government check or US postal money order
State or local government check
A bank, certified, or traveler's check
A check from your own bank
A check from a local bank
A check from a regional bank
A check from an out-of-state bank

Routing numbers appear in **magnetic image character recognition code (MICR)** in the bottom left hand corner of your check. The first set is the code for your bank and the second set is your account number. Scanning machines read the code and forward the data to the right location. If you ever need to arrange a wire transfer of money from one account to another, you'll need to provide the bank and account routing numbers.

day that you make the request and is available in the recipient's account the next day. You can also establish wire transfer privileges between a mutual fund and your bank, as long as the two accounts are registered exactly the same way. Typically, the transferred money is available the next day. If the fund is handling the transfer, there's usually no fee.

Stop payment orders are instructions you give your bank telling it not to pay a specific check that you've written. There's generally a fee comparable to the fee for bouncing a check. But you can prevent payment on a check that has been lost and perhaps stolen or on a check for goods or services that are defective or unacceptable. You can give the order over the phone, but should provide a written request as well.

A **wire transfer** is a fast way to move money electronically from one account to another. For a fee, you can ask your bank to send money from your account to someone else's, provided you have the account number and bank routing number. Usually, the transaction goes through at the end of the business

CHECKING UP
Retailers selling large-ticket items sometimes require a bank check as a guarantee they'll get their money. That's because if a personal check bounces or you put a stop payment order on it, retailers can't charge the purchase price to a credit card you might have left for identification (although they can go after you for the money in court).

But once you've delivered a bank check, the bill is paid.

on is located, and the amount. Banks may require you to use a special deposit slip for one-day clearing and may process ATM deposits more slowly than deposits with a teller. And checks from international banks may take up to a month to clear.

Here's a typical schedule for a $1,000 deposit. You can check with your bank for the schedule it uses.

1 day later*	2 days later*	3 days later*	6 days later*
$1,000			
$1,000			
$1,000			
$1,000			
$100	$400	$500	
$100		$900	
$100			$900

* The number of days refers to business days.

25

What Works for You

If you're like most people, you work to live. So you want to find a type of work that fits your life.

Even if you've had jobs before—back in high school, during summers, or at college—working for a living, when you're living on your own and taking care of yourself, has a different feel to it. Chances are you'll be spending more time doing your job than you ever have before, and the money you make will probably be a lot more important to you.

That's why it's so important to make sure that you're doing something that's right for you. And finding that job often means more than just doing something you enjoy. Sure, what you do as work has a huge impact on your day-to-day satisfaction, but *how* you do it—your work schedule, your relationship with your employer, your job security, and other elements—can be just as important.

FULL-TIME

KEEP YOUR OPTIONS OPEN

For many people, a traditional **full-time job** fits their lifestyle and their needs. After all, there's something nice about knowing you've got steady employment. And the benefits that often come with it, like health insurance and retirement savings plans, can provide security as well.

But getting a full-time job is only one of several ways to work. And while it can provide for your needs pretty well, it doesn't fit everybody's lifestyle. Other styles of work can provide freedom and variety that you won't find at a 9-to-5 job.

> **TIME FOR A CHANGE**
> **The average person holds 9.2 jobs between ages 18 and 34.**
> That means making a change about once every 20 months. More than half of those changes usually happen before age 24.

WORKING PART-TIME

For example, if you've got a passion that takes up a lot of your time—anything from writing the Great American Novel, to caring for your family or starting your own business—a **part-time job** can be a great way to support yourself along the way.

Traditional day jobs, like waiting tables or working in retail, can give you a more open and flexible schedule—even if it sometimes means you'll be working at night rather than during the day. And if you get good tips or work a lot of overtime hours, you can make quite a lot of money this way. You might find yourself missing out on benefits, though. Unless you're working for a fairly established company, chances are you won't be getting things like health insurance, retirement savings, or paid time off.

PART-TIME FULL-TIME

While it's not quite as common, it's certainly possible to find a part-time position at a more traditional job. For example, you might be able to work four days a week, or have several mornings or afternoons off. The only downside is that unless you've got job skills that are in high demand, chances are you'll earn much less than a full-time employee doing the same job. You'll also be more vulnerable to layoffs if business isn't going well.

But in a strong job market, part-time workers are often valued as highly as their full-time counterparts, and the salary reductions are usually proportionate and fair, even when you're earning a fixed salary for your hours. For example, if you want to work a four-day week, which is 80% of a full five-day schedule, many employers will offer you 80% of a full-time salary.

Some employers offer full benefits as long as you work a certain number of hours per week, while others will pay an appropriate portion of the cost. Whatever the case, you'll be making less than you would for full-time work, but if you have other priorities outside of your day job, it may be worth it to you.

FOOTLOOSE AND FANCY-FREELANCING

Lots of people, especially young people, find that **freelance** or **contract-based** work fits well with the lives they want to lead. Just about every industry employs contract workers, from computer programming to landscaping. And if you've got skills that are in demand, you can command a price that will often bring you more money than full-time, on-staff employees earn. Of course you've got to be the one to line up your own work, and that can be difficult to do if you don't have a lot of contacts, or if the economy is in a downturn.

PART-TIME

FREELANCE

TEMPING

If you're between jobs, or just taking some time to decide on your career path, **temporary employment** can be a great way to get exposure while you earn money. In recent years, temping has expanded from mostly clerical work to a way to try your hand at skilled work in a wide variety of different fields. And just as with other types of work, the more skilled the position you're qualified for, the more you're likely to be paid.

If you want to temp, you typically enroll with an employment agency. When you do, you effectively become that company's employee, and it hires you out to other companies. Working through an agency has its plusses and minuses. On one hand, the agency takes care of many of the business issues that temps have to deal with on their own. It may even cover some or all of your benefits. But since the agency has to make money too, you won't get paid as much as direct employees of the companies where you work.

TEMP

> When I started out at my first real job, I had no idea of what the average daily schedule was like at my new office. I wanted to make a good impression, so I was afraid to leave my desk for lunch, even though I was working well more than the required hours. I ended up not eating for the first week—I couldn't even bring myself to take the food I brought from home out of my bag.
>
> —Sarah S., 24

Getting Down to Business

You can't chart your career path exactly. But if you know how different types of jobs measure up on different issues, you'll have a better sense of where you stand.

No job is perfect. There are real advantages and some serious drawbacks to most of them—whether you're on a full-time career path, trying to make it as a freelancer, or temping just enough hours to pay your bills. But don't feel trapped: Experiment with various ways to work until you find the one that is right for you.

FACTORS	HOURS	FLEXIBILITY	PAY STYLE	BENEFITS 
FULL-TIME	35-50 hours is a typical work week	Often it's limited, but a growing number of companies offer flex time	Most office jobs pay on a salaried basis. Many other jobs—and some clerical office jobs—pay on an hourly basis	Many employers offer health insurance, and many offer a retirement savings plan, often with matching funds
PART-TIME	Service jobs may vary depending on seniority, and may include overtime. Office jobs may be a percentage of full-time hours—such as half-time—or set at 10 or 20 hours a week	You may be able to select hours that fit your lifestyle, but in some service jobs you may have to work evenings and weekends	Service jobs usually pay hourly, often with higher pay for overtime. Office jobs may pay a salary or hourly rate	To be eligible for health coverage, you've usually got to work at least 30 hours a week, and you may have to pay to participate. If you're eligible for a retirement plan, you've usually got to work at least 1,000 hours a year to participate
FREELANCE	Your time varies with each job or client and the amount of work required	You may be able to select hours that fit your life-style, but you also may have to cater more to your clients' needs	Some jobs pay on an hourly basis, while some pay a flat rate	You have to pay for your own health coverage and manage your own retirement savings plan
TEMP	You may work anywhere from a few hours a day to full-time	You might have to adapt to the assignment you're given, but most agencies will try to find a position that fits your needs and skills	Usually on an hourly basis	Some agencies provide health coverage, but many don't

FLEX YOUR MUSCLES

If you want to work full- or part-time, but still have some control over exactly which hours you work, you've got an increasingly good chance of getting your way. More than a quarter of employees work at jobs with **flexible work schedules**, or **flex time**, which allows them to control when they start and finish their work day. Flex time may not be available if you're in a first job or an entry-level position, but if it's available, it can be a great way to make a position more manageable, or smooth your transition into the working world.

VACATIONS	JOB SECURITY	TAXES AND WITHHOLDING	VARIETY
Salaried jobs usually offer paid vacations—at most places, you earn your time for the first year and get two weeks or more in subsequent years	While nothing is guaranteed, your job is more secure than many other types Some employers offer contracts securing your position for a set amount of time	Your employer withholds money from your paycheck for taxes based on what you indicate on your W-4	You may get a variety of different tasks or projects, but you'll be working for one employer in one industry
Permanent part-time employees at office jobs may qualify for paid time off	As long as you're a satisfactory employee, you're fairly secure, although in a bad economy you may be laid off before full-time employees	Your company withholds money from your paycheck for taxes according to what you indicate on your W-4	You may get a variety of different tasks or projects, but you'll be working for one employer in one industry
You've got to cover yourself financially if you want to take time off, and it may mean missing out on jobs	You're responsible for securing your own work	You'll have to be responsible for paying your own taxes, usually by paying estimated taxes on a quarterly basis You'll have to pay twice as much to Social Security and Medicare	Depending on your skills, you can work for as many companies in as many industries as you can find
You've got to cover yourself financially if you want to take time off	You can request to be placed with specific companies, but you're not in control of when or how much you work You may be able to move up to a permanent position, but there's no guarantee	Most agencies will take care of withholding for you as a direct employer would	You can work for a number of different companies, but your choices are bound by what your agency can provide

The Total Package

There's more to compensation than just getting paid.

Chances are your salary will be your biggest concern when you're choosing among jobs or negotiating a compensation package with your new employer. After all, regular income is the most basic priority. If you don't have enough to pay for essentials like rent, food, and clothing, benefits like a retirement savings plan and even health insurance might seem unimportant. But it pays to consider a wide variety of benefits.

While most employers offer full-time employees a package of benefits, some are more comprehensive than others. When you're looking at jobs, make sure you weigh the different benefits, and make the best overall package, not just the highest salary, your ultimate priority. That way you can be sure you've got all your bases covered—for the present as well as the future.

INSURANCE

Health insurance is by far the most common job benefit, as well as the most popular. And with good reason: Even if you have to pay part of the cost out of every paycheck, the protection that health insurance provides is more than worth the cost—even if you need it only once.

Even if you're usually healthy and you use health insurance just for regular checkups, it's still better to have it than not. Without insurance, it would take just one serious injury or emergency operation to put a huge hole in your financial security.

RETIREMENT PLANS

Retirement plans are another popular benefit, and one you should make a priority when you're evaluating different employers. Retirement might seem a long way off when you're just getting started, but if you can't plan on a source of income after you stop working, retirement may be a lot further away—or less enjoyable—than you'd like it to be.

Employer sponsored retirement plans, whether funded entirely by your employer, by you alone, or by you and your employer together, offer an easy and effective way to start preparing for the future.

MAKE YOUR OWN BENEFITS: CAFETERIA PLANS

Some employers let you have a hand in designing your own benefits package by offering **cafeteria plans**, more formally known as **flexible spending plans**. These plans may include several **core benefits**, such as health insurance or a retirement savings plan.

But they also let you set aside pretax income, which you can allocate among the plan options your employer offers to pay for certain expenses. For example, you could put money into a cafeteria plan to cover extra life insurance, uninsured medical expenses, such as prescription glasses or contacts, or childcare if you need it. As the bills for those expenses come due, you can use the money you've put into the plan to pay for them.

Cafeteria plans can be a great opportunity to tailor your benefits package to your needs. And since the amounts you

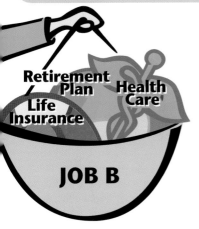

put aside reduce your taxable income, you actually end up with more money in your pocket than if you didn't participate. The catch is that you have to plan carefully to be sure you'll spend the full amount you allocate on eligible expenses before the end of the year. If you don't spend it, you can't get it back.

For example, if you set aside $1,500 for medical expenses but you only spend $1,000, you lose the other $500. One solution is to buy an extra pair of glasses or speed up some optional dental work.

EXTRA PROTECTION

While it's one of the most common job benefits, health coverage is just the beginning when it comes to insurance. Many employers offer **disability insurance** and **life insurance** as part of cafeteria plans, and some might even provide them as elements of regular benefits packages. Or you might be considering buying one of these policies on your own.

BENEFITS FOR COUPLES

If you're married or have a domestic partner, it makes sense to think of your benefits packages together, and try to get the best *overall* package between the two of you. Here are just a few ways to get the most out of your compensation packages:

Share the health. If your partner gets employee health coverage that will cover you, it's smart to use his or her plan if it provides better coverage than what's available to you—and vice versa, of course. If your plan is better, it makes sense for you to stick with it, even if you can't cover anyone else under it.

One good thing about being covered under someone else's plan is that it can give you a little freedom if you're currently looking for a job, or thinking about freelancing or working in some other situation where you won't have coverage from an employer.

Invest in one another. If one of you has a better retirement plan than the other, you might want to put more of that person's salary into the plan and devote more of the other person's earnings to more immediate short-term expenses.

If you're not earning income at all—if you're going to school, say, or taking care of a child—your spouse can open a **spousal IRA** and invest money in your name, and vice versa, if you're working but your spouse is not.

Serve each other. If both of you have a cafeteria plan at work, you can save even more by picking and choosing benefits. For example, you could set aside money for optical coverage under your own plan, and let your spouse set aside money for childcare.

Each state and employer has its own rules and policies about domestic partners. Make sure you know what you're eligible for before you make any decisions.

Whether these added forms of protection are worth the money—from what you've set aside of your salary for cafeteria benefits or straight from your wallet—depends on your own situation. Many young people don't feel like they have much that would need protecting if they died or were suddenly disabled. But if you're supporting a family, or paying a mortgage, you might want to think about taking these kinds of precautions.

Bonus Benefits

Extra benefits can move you ahead in life—but they can also be a roll of the dice.

With some employers, traditional benefits, such as health coverage and retirement plans, are just the beginning. In fact, it's not uncommon to find benefits packages that include anything and everything from stock options to day care services.

These extra benefits can be strong incentives to take one job over another, but don't lose sight of the bigger picture. Ask yourself objectively if you really need the incentives these companies are offering—and if they outweigh the less glamorous but more important opportunities you might have at other jobs.

OPTIONS WITH OPTIONS

Some employers offer **stock options** as part of compensation packages or instead of cash bonuses. These options give you the right to buy the company's stock at a set price, called a **strike price**. In certain cases—if the publicly traded stock rises substantially in value, or if a privately held company is acquired or goes public—exercising your options and selling the stock may put a lot of money in your pocket, even after taxes.

But that's not always the case. After all, no stock's price is a sure bet. You could easily end up **underwater**. That means you're gasping for air—figuratively speaking—when the current price of your company

stock is lower than your strike price. That makes the options worthless, since you'd pay more to exercise them than to buy shares on the open market.

In addition, many companies require you to work for a set period of time in order to become fully **vested**, or entitled to all the options you're being offered. That can trap you with what are known as **golden handcuffs**, meaning you're tied to a job you'd otherwise leave because you want to collect on the options you were promised.

Similarly, if your company goes public, there may be restrictions on when you can sell the stock you get by exercising your options. You'll also want to think twice if options come at the expense of a larger salary. While options may pay off big down the road, they can also end up being a bust.

SHARING THE BENEFITS

Many privately held companies have no immediate plans to go public, but still want to let you share in the profits if the company increases in value. In some cases, they'll offer **stock appreciation rights (SARs)** instead of options.

Like stock options, SARs offer promises, not guarantees, of future benefit. Depending on how your

BONUS POINTS

If you sign an employment contract with certain companies, you may get an up-front bonus, often several thousand dollars or more. Extra cash like this can be a huge help in dealing with the costs of moving or setting up a new apartment, or for a summer trip or other last hurrah before you start work. But make sure you're comfortable with the contract you're signing before you let a bonus reel you in. If you break its terms—by leaving the company earlier than you initially agree to, for example—you might end up having to give that money back.

QUALITY-OF-LIFE BENEFITS

Most employee benefits are financial, but some companies also offer perks that can improve your lifestyle rather than your bank account. These benefits generally fall into two categories.

The first group can make your life better in the long run even if you don't expect to take advantage of them right away. For example, some companies offer paid leave if a child or parent is sick. Others may offer a sabbatical break if you've been working there for a while. Or they might pay for a graduate degree.

employer's plan is set up, you might be paid the difference between the value of the stock at the time you received your SARs and the value at what's known as a **triggering event**—a sale, an **initial public offering (IPO)**, or your leaving the company. Or you might be able to convert your SARs to stock options at some point.

One big difference, from your perspective, is that with SARs you don't need to purchase stock in order to benefit from an increase in value. The corresponding downside is that once you collect on SARs, you don't benefit from any potential future gains in the stock's value since you get a cash payout and not the actual stock. But you also aren't exposed to potential losses if the stock declines in value in the future.

Some companies also offer benefits geared toward making your day-to-day life a little more manageable. This can mean anything from a subsidized on-site cafeteria to a free concierge service that can pick up your dry cleaning and water your plants. If you want to make your transition into real-life responsibility a little easier, these perks can certainly help. But make sure they're are really worthwhile—especially when you take into account that most companies that provide these benefits do so because they want you to spend more of your time and energy at work.

LET THE GOOD TIMES ROLL

The stronger the economy is, the more likely employers are to offer incentives. Some companies, especially those in thriving, competitive industries, may offer benefits that are more than a few notches above the usual insurance and retirement choices—anything from pet health insurance to use of corporate vacation facilities.

If you're hired when times are tighter, the wooing may be a little less ardent. But in the next economic upswing, be prepared to argue that existing employees should be offered at least as many perks as new recruits.

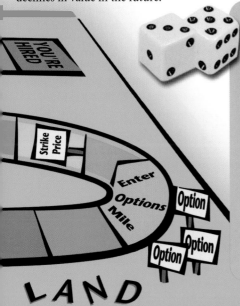

The Fine Print

Make sure you know what you're getting into before you sign on the dotted line.

Taking a job can mean a lot more than just agreeing to show up every morning. Your employer may require you to sign a contract or other agreement that very specifically governs what you can say and do while you're at the company—or after you leave.

Although there's not a lot you can do to avoid signing if it's a job you want, it's important to recognize the potential consequences if you agree to certain terms and conditions. That way you can be prepared for some of the situations you might encounter.

Sign here:

X - - - - -

NDA: KEEPING SECRETS

The first agreement you're likely to come across is a **non-disclosure agreement (NDA)**, sometimes called a **confidentiality agreement**. By signing an NDA when you're hired, you agree not to share any of a company's proprietary information with people outside the company, both during and after the time you're employed.

Of course, what is and isn't proprietary information depends on whose information it is. At some companies, you're simply prohibited from talking about new products or ventures that haven't been made public yet. But other, more competitive employers insist on much more control over what you learn and create while you're on the job. In some extreme cases, you might have to sign an NDA at a job interview, before you even find out what a company really does.

NON-COMPETE AGREEMENTS

Some companies might also include a **non-compete agreement** in your contract or job offer letter. These clauses mean that if you accept their offer, you're restricted from working for competitors for a certain period of time after you leave. Other employers ask you to sign non-compete agreements when you're laid off if you want to be entitled to **severance pay**.

Many people feel that non-compete clauses are inherently unfair. After all, unless you're deliberately planning to change career paths, not being allowed to work for other companies in the same industry can severely limit your future job prospects. Fortunately, most courts feel the same way, and non-compete agreements rarely hold up in court, especially those that extend their control for long periods of time or over large geographic areas.

Nevertheless, many companies use them as scare tactics, hoping that

INSIDER TRADING

If you're working for or with a public company whose shares are traded on the stock markets, make sure you know the story on **insider trading**. That's when corporate officers, or other people who might have access to confidential information, buy or sell the company's stock. If this trading decision is based on information that's not available to the public, it's illegal. So is passing on that information to anyone who buys or sells based on it.

Just because you're not a corporate officer or a major stockholder doesn't mean you don't run the risk of getting caught up in illegal insider trading. Anyone with access to corporate information could potentially get in trouble. For example, if you're a paralegal at a corporate law firm, the information you see and hear about clients could be used for insider trading.

Or if you work at a newspaper or other periodical, you could trade on information you learn before it goes out on the newsstands. And if you share this information with anyone, you could both end up in jail. So if you're in a work situation where you've got access to private corporate information, watch what you do and say.

you'll comply with their conditions just because you've signed their agreements. And some employers do take legal action if you break the agreement. So while you shouldn't let a non-compete agreement deter you from exploring other job opportunities, be forewarned that there may be consequences.

MONEY TALKS

It's perfectly natural to be curious about what your coworkers are earning. And it can be enlightening to see what you're being paid compared to what veteran employees and other rookies are making.

The personnel office or your supervisor might suggest subtly—or not so subtly—that you should keep your salary to yourself. While you should certainly be discreet, it's illegal for them to forbid you to discuss it.

Getting Paid

Your paycheck gets star billing, but your paystub tells you what goes on behind the scenes.

No matter how long you work, or how many paychecks you get, you'll probably never quite get over the shock of coming face-to-face with the difference between what you earn and the amount you take home—or have deposited in your checking account.

NOTHING BUT NET

What you end up with, after all the deductions are withheld, is your **net pay** for the period, more commonly known as your **take-home pay**. Even if the person who works next to you has the same gross pay, chances are your checks will be for different amounts.

That's because to calculate net pay, your employer subtracts each employee's taxes and benefits. How much gets taken out depends on several things:

- The elective benefits you participate in and how much you contribute
- How many allowances you claim on the W-4 form you filled out when you started work
- Where you live

If your co-worker put more or less money than you did into a retirement savings plan, had more dependents or a second job so took a different number of allowances, or lived in an income-taxing city while you lived in the suburbs, your checks could be for substantially different amounts.

Your paystub usually has a section with all of your relevant **personal information**, including your name and address, Social Security number, marital status, and any employer-specific information.

EARNINGS STATEMENT

BIG CORPORATION
123 BROADWAY
ANYTOWN, AW 11110

JIM MILLER
42 HILLTOP RD
ANYTOWN, AW 11134

Social Security Number:	123-45-6789
Department Number:	071
Marital Status:	SINGLE
Number of Allowances:	02

Gross pay is the amount you earned for the pay period. If you're paid by the hour, the number of hours and the hourly rate will be provided. If you've received any pay other than salary or wages, such as bonuses or commissions, those amounts will appear on separate lines. There'll also be a year-to-date total for each category.

GROSS PAY YEAR TO DATE	GROSS PAY THIS
16000.00	2000.
TOTAL DEDUCTIONS THIS PERIOD	NET PAY TH
655.00	134

BIG CORPORATION
123 BROADWAY
ANYTOWN, AW 11110

$1,345.00 DEPOSI

Pay To
The Order Of

JIM
42
AN

····· VOID····· VOID···

If you use **direct deposit**, what looks like a check will be attached to the paystub for your reference. But since the money will already be in your account, the image will be voided so that you can't deposit it—unfortunately.

USING THE BOSS' BANK

If your employer has its accounts with a certain bank, you might consider using that bank too. You may qualify for free checking, a small reduction in borrowing costs, or a credit card with no annual fee.

A direct connection between bank and employer can make any problems you have a lot easier to resolve.

But if you can get better or cheaper banking somewhere else, those advantages are likely to outweigh the convenience of using your employer's bank.

The **pay period** identifies the days or weeks the check covers. If you're paid twice a month, the check you get on the 15th may cover the first half of the current month or the last half of the previous month.

Pay Period: 01/01 to 01/15
Pay Date: 01/30

HOURS AND EARNINGS		
	THIS PERIOD	YEAR-TO-DATE
HOURS	2000.00	16000.00

TAXES AND DEDUCTIONS			
DEDUCTION	THIS PERIOD	YEAR-TO-DATE	
401K	100.00		401K
FICA	100.00		FICA
FEW WT	300.00		FEW WT
AW ST	100.00		AW ST
AW DIS	5.00		AW DIS
Any Town	50.00		Any Town
FED WT	300.00		FED WT

DEPOSIT

Check Date: 01/30/02

K# 111000099 CHK ACCT# 111000088 $1,345.00

AD
W 11134

Withholding and **deductions** are subtracted from your gross pay to prepay federal income taxes, state and local income taxes if you owe them, and Social Security and Medicare taxes (sometimes lumped together as **FICA**, for **Federal Insurance Contributions Act**). Health insurance premiums, retirement savings plan or flexible spending plan contributions, union dues, or prepaid transportation may also be withheld.

DIRECT DEPOSIT

If you want easy, fast access to your paycheck, go for **direct deposit**. You just fill out a short form and give your employer a voided check. It's that simple.

Every time you get paid, the money is deposited electronically in your account on the day checks are issued. If the official pay date falls on a weekend, your check may even be deposited at the end of the day on Friday.

Depending on your bank's policy, your money may be available immediately, and it's always available by the next day at the latest. And since banks like the electronic ease of direct deposit, they'll sometimes even reduce your checking account fees if you sign up for it.

Direct deposit can also be a great way to keep on top of your investing plans since you can have each check split up and deposited into more than one account. If you have part of your pay go right into an investment account, you can be sure that you're contributing regularly without having to think about it.

THE SILVER LINING

It might seem like having all of that money sucked out of your gross pay is bad news, especially since so much goes toward paying taxes. But if you're putting money into a retirement savings plan or a flexible spending account, there may be quite a lot to smile about.

That's because that money comes out before your income taxes are withheld. Subtracting it reduces the taxes you owe and the amount that's withheld to pay them. So even though your net pay is reduced by your contributions, the benefits cost you less than they would if you had to pay for them out of your net pay. And that is likely to mean more money in your pocket in the long run.

Meet Your 401(k)

If you're lucky enough to be introduced to a 401(k), you'll make a friend for life.

Even if you're just starting your first real job—actually, *especially* if you're just starting your first real job—it's time to start thinking about retiring. That's not a comment on how motivated—or unmotivated—you are, or a suggestion that you should wish your life away. It's just reality.

That's because you, like many people, will be responsible for supporting yourself during the 30 or 40 years you can expect to live after you retire. To do that, you need a source of income that will stretch further than the safety net of Social Security and be more reliable than winning the lottery.

Some—but increasingly few—employers offer traditional pensions, which pay you retirement income based on your final salary and time on the job. Others contribute to a cash balance, profit sharing, or other plan on your behalf. But most employers offer you, instead, the opportunity to participate in a **tax-deferred salary reduction** plan, such as a **401(k)**.

BRIGHT AND EARLY

To show the impact of starting to invest as early as you can in a 401(k) or other retirement savings plan, compare the potential results if you began investing at different points in your working life. To keep matters simple, assume your employer doesn't match your contributions and you put in the same amount each year you participate.

Remember that returns are not guaranteed. Your return could be low, and you could lose as well as make money.

20 years of contributions

401(k) PLAN I started at age 45

401(k) PLAN I started at age 35

30 years of contributions

My contribution	$100,000
Annual return	8%
Account value	$247,114.61

You decide to enjoy the money you have while you're young, and you don't start contributing to your 401(k) until you're 45. If you contribute $5,000 a year and average an 8% annual return, you'll have about $247,000 in your account if you stop contributing at 65, based on a total contribution of $100,00.

My contribution	$150,000
Annual return	8%
Account value	$611,729.34

When you reach 35, you realize it's time to get serious about the future, so you start contributing $5,000 a year to your 401(k). Your investment return averages 8% a year. When you retire at 65, your account value will be about $611,000, based on a total contribution of $150,000.

Race for the Prize: A More

ON THE BANDWAGON

If your employer offers a salary reduction plan, it's usually the most painless way to set aside money for the future. All you have to do is agree to have a percentage of your gross income withheld each pay period and added to the money already invested in your plan account.

Participating in a salary reduction plan has three big advantages:

Your tax-deferred contributions reduce your current income taxes since they're subtracted from your income before tax withholding is calculated. Think of it as getting a reward for making a smart decision.

Many employers match a percentage of the contributions you make—as close to a free lunch as you're likely to get, since you don't owe income tax now on that amount either.

Any earnings in your retirement accumulate tax deferred. That means the earnings are reinvested to increase the base on which additional earnings can accumulate, a process called **compounding**.

WHY NOW?

When **compounding** is involved, time is money. The more years that you add contributions to your plan, and the more years that any earnings increase your principal, the larger your account balance has the potential to grow.

Of course, there are no guarantees about either the rate or the regularity of the earnings. They may be outstanding one year and dismal the next, or they may go through longer, but still alternating, periods of growth and decline. That's the reality of investing. Having time on your side means that bumps in the road, like a period when investment prices go down and your account value shrinks, may be setbacks. But they don't have to be fatal.

My contribution	$200,000
Annual return	8%
Account value	**$1,398,905.20**

You start contributing to a 401(k) at 25, as soon as you're eligible for a plan. You contribute $5,000 a year for 40 years until you retire at 65. Your return averages 8%, so your account value is almost $1.4 million, based on a total contribution of $200,000.

Secure Retirement

A 401(k) BY ANY OTHER NAME...

401(k) plans are the most common, and best known, employer sponsored salary reduction plans. But they're not the only ones. If you work for a not-for-profit organization such as a school or college, a hospital, a cultural institution, or a charitable organization, your employer may offer a **403(b) plan**, sometimes known as a **tax-deferred annuity (TDA)**.

Similarly, the plan a state or municipal government offers may be a **457 plan,** while federal government departments and agencies provide a **thrift savings plan.** And if you work for a small company—one with fewer than 100 employees—you may be part of a **SIMPLE plan**, an acronym for **Savings Incentive Match Plan for Employees**.

The rules differ slightly for each type of plan, and even among plans of the same type. But all offer the opportunity for tax deferral.

401(k) Mix and Match

It can take some trial and error to find the right 401(k) formula.

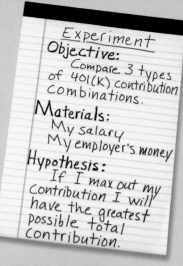

Experiment
Objective:
Compare 3 types of 401(k) contribution combinations.
Materials:
My salary
My employer's money
Hypothesis:
If I max out my contribution I will have the greatest possible total contribution.

If you want to contribute to a salary reduction plan, but you're feeling confused, you're not alone. Even the parts that are fairly easy to do—including deferring current income into your plan—aren't always easy to understand.

That's true in part because some fairly complicated federal rules govern these plans. And each employer's plan is a little different from every other one.

PLAYING THE PERCENTAGES

There's no one answer to the question of how much to contribute to your 401(k) or 403(b) plan. In fact, the answers you get may seem contradictory.

The federal government caps the dollar amount you can contribute in any one year. For 2005, that limit is $14,000, increasing to $15,000 in 2006 for all plans but SIMPLEs, where the cap is $10,000. All caps may be adjusted upward in the future.

Your employer may put a separate ceiling on your contribution, typically at a percentage of what you earn. Those limits typically run between 10% and 20%, depending on the employer, with 15% being the most common.

You can see why things get confusing. There may be two different limits, one set by the government, and one by your employer. And what happens when the two limits conflict because the government permits a higher contribution than your employer, or the other way around? The lower limit prevails.

And remember, some employers require you to contribute at least 1% or 2% of your earnings to participate in the program, though the government doesn't have a minimum.

HOW MATCHING WORKS

Employers who elect to match some or all of their employees' contributions can set their own rules for how this program operates. One typical approach is for the employer to match

A TEST CASE

Suppose you earn $50,000, and you're eligible to contribute to your employer's 401(k) plan. Your employer caps contributions at 15%. So the most you can contribute is $7,500, or $312.50 every paycheck if you get paid twice a month.

If you put away that much, you're afraid that you won't be able to cover your rent, food, student loan payments, and all the other things you spend money on.

Could you do half that amount, or $156.25 every two weeks? That may be more doable, since reducing your taxable salary by $3,750 means that about $1,000 less

Your contribution

Employer's contribution

Total contribution

50% of what an employee contributes, up to a maximum of 6% of earnings.

Using that example, if you earned $40,000 and contributed 6% of your salary, or $2,400 to a 401(k), your employer would add $1,200. That's 50% of 6%. Even if you contributed 10% of your salary, the same employer would still contribute $1,200, or 50% of 6%.

But if you contributed only 4% of your salary, or $1,600, your employer would add $800, or 50% of your contribution.

MATCH POINT

Even if you've mastered the rules on contribution limits and the various ways matching contributions are handled, it's still easy to get

YOUR EMPLOYER

YOU

is withheld for federal income taxes. So you'll only be short $2,750 for the year.

Plus your employer will match 50% of your contribution up to 6% of your salary. That's another $62.50 a pay period going into your retirement account, or $1,500 total. So by the end of the year, $5,250 will have been added to your account.

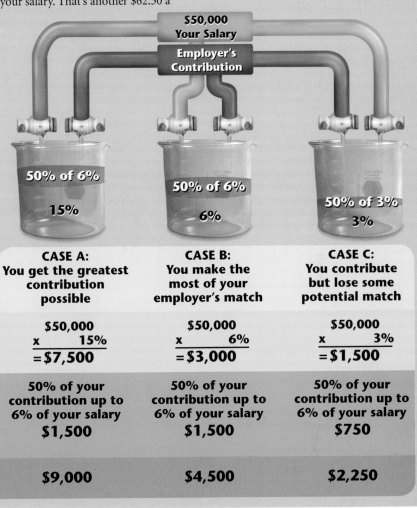

$50,000 **Your Salary**		
Employer's **Contribution**		
50% of 6% **15%**	50% of 6% **6%**	50% of 3% **3%**
CASE A: **You get the greatest** **contribution** **possible**	**CASE B:** **You make the** **most of your** **employer's match**	**CASE C:** **You contribute** **but lose some** **potential match**
$50,000 x 15% = **$7,500**	$50,000 x 6% = **$3,000**	$50,000 x 3% = **$1,500**
50% of your contribution up to 6% of your salary **$1,500**	50% of your contribution up to 6% of your salary **$1,500**	50% of your contribution up to 6% of your salary **$750**
$9,000	**$4,500**	**$2,250**

confused about how much you should put away. While there's no one answer for everyone, many experts say that you should max out, contributing up to your employer's or the government's cap, whichever kicks in first.

If that's a higher amount than you can afford, most experts agree that you should contribute as much as you can. And if your employer matches a percentage of what you contribute, you should put in at least enough to qualify for the maximum match. Since the matching contribution is essentially free money, you don't want to miss out on it.

On the other hand, if your employer doesn't match your contribution, or the investment choices that your plan offers are limited, you might decide to contribute the maximum to an **individual retirement account (IRA)**, perhaps a tax-free **Roth IRA**. You can invest as you choose, and you may be able to move your IRA savings into another employer's plan in the future.

FLEXIBLE LIMITS

If your employer matches part of your retirement savings contribution, that amount doesn't count toward the government's dollar limit. Nor does it reduce the percentage of earnings you're allowed to contribute. The only catch is that while you are vested immediately in your contribution, you probably will have to stay on the job a number of years to be fully vested in your employer's contribution. When you're vested and change employers, you can take the plan assets with you.

Making 401(k) Decisions

Your 401(k)plan offers a wide menu of choices. But you've got to serve yourself.

The point of investing in a 401(k) now, when you know that you won't realize the benefits for 30 or 40 years, is that you have the opportunity to amass a tidy sum.

In the 25 or so years that 401(k) plans have been in existence, many people have been able to accumulate accounts of substantial value despite sometimes dramatic drops in the overall investment market. The key is to maintain a long-term perspective. Realizing an average annual return of 8% a year for 30 years can produce significant gains.

Of course, that doesn't happen automatically. You've got to allocate your assets and diversify your portfolio. That means deciding how your contribution is invested by selecting from among the investments your 401(k) plan offers.

WHAT THE CHOICES ARE

Mutual funds are the most common entrées on 401(k) menus. Most plans offer a range of funds, including **stock funds**, **bond funds**, and **money market funds**, as well as **balanced funds** that invest in both stocks and bonds. **Index funds**, which invest to reproduce the performance of a particular market index, are also typical. You might also find a few more specialized funds, such as one that invests in international stocks, or one that focuses on up-and-coming small companies.

Some plans concentrate on **variable annuities**, sometimes identified as **separate accounts** or **annuity accounts**. And an increasing number of 401(k) plans—but not 403(b)s or 457s—offer **brokerage accounts**, also known as **brokerage windows**, that allow you to purchase individual stocks and bonds as well as mutual funds from dozens of different companies.

SLICING THE PIE

Since you've got the time to weather the ups and downs of the stock market, you may want to consider putting up to 80% of your contributions in different types of stock funds, including stock index funds, that have the potential to increase in value over the long term.

401(k) ENTRÉES

INDEX INTER-NATIONAL BALANCED

STOCKS BONDS MONEY MARKET

COMPANY STOCK
Your employer might include company stock as an investment option in your 401(k) plan. If it's a great company, the stock can be a smart choice. But you may also risk being too dependent on the fortunes of a single company. Get some independent advice before you decide.

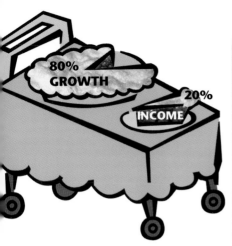

80% GROWTH

20% INCOME

These funds may lose value more quickly than a **balanced fund** that buys a mix of stocks and bonds, which tend to react differently to changes in the economy or the investment markets. But remember that stock funds may increase in value more dramatically as well. That's why spreading your risk is so important.

You may want to split the rest of your 401(k) money between **income** investments and those designed to provide **stability**, sometimes described as preservation of principal. For example, you might choose a bond fund to provide a stream of interest that can be reinvested to buy additional shares of the fund. And since different investment classes perform well at different times, those bond funds may provide a better return when stocks are doing badly.

Stable value funds usually invest in money markets and other highly secure investments, which generally don't have a lot of potential for growth or earnings. It's often a good idea to put a little money into stability funds. But remember that you should be doing it for the sake of diversity and security, not for any large gain.

GO YOUR OWN WAY

While most young people select a 401(k) portfolio like the one described above—fairly aggressive, based mostly on growth-oriented stocks and funds—that's not the only way to structure your investments. If you're just not comfortable taking that kind of risk, think about putting a little more of your contribution into equity income or growth and income funds.

O if you've got a trust or a taxable investment portfolio that will provide you with money for retirement, it's perfectly reasonable to rethink how you want to split up, or **allocate**, your 401(k).

No matter which investment route you take, the most important thing to do is to get started. Don't tell yourself

401(k) TO GO

If you change jobs, your 401(k) is **portable**. That means your contributions and whatever they've earned are yours to keep. And if you've been at your job long enough, your employer's matching contributions are yours too.

You may be able to transfer what you've got to a new employer's plan, and you can always put it in an IRA if your new employer doesn't have a plan or doesn't allow you to transfer money from your old one.

What you don't want to do when you change jobs is take the money out of your retirement savings plan and spend it. First of all, you'll owe income tax on the lump sum—which you might have to pay at a higher rate if the amount propels you into a new tax bracket. You'll also owe a 10% penalty on the entire amount of the withdrawal. And perhaps worst of all, you'll have to start all over again to build a retirement account.

If your account balance is between $1,000 and $5,000 when you leave your job, your employer must roll the money into an IRA unless you provide other instructions. You'll be notified where it is, and you have the right to move it. If the balance is less than $1,000, your employer has the right to cash you out, or send you a check for the balance minus 20% that must be withheld for income tax.

Even if that happens, you can put the money (plus the withheld 20% from some other source if you've got it) into a rollover IRA within 60 days and hold onto its tax-deferred status. If you don't qualify to join your new employer's plan until you've been on the job for a year, money you've moved to an IRA can continue to accumulate tax-deferred earnings. And you may make your annual IRA contribution to that account.

you'll start investing, contributing, or allocating your contributions more aggressively, sometime in the future. Even if you do eventually follow through on it, you'll be missing out on money you could be earning now.

Health Insurance

Many employers provide a good shield against medical costs.

When you're young and healthy, it's hard to be too worried about illness or injury. The aches and pains your parents and grandparents complain about are decades away. Injuries and accidents are things that happen to other people.

But what if you *do* get sick or hurt? The reality is that you're never immune. And being sick can be very expensive. A typical hospital stay can cost thousands of dollars a day, and even a visit to the doctor averages well over $100.

That's where employer sponsored health insurance comes in. It can help cover many of the healthcare expenses you might be faced with—usually doctor and hospital visits, prescription drugs, and sometimes dental care, mental healthcare, and physical therapy. And many insurance plans cover preventative care, including annual check-ups, as well.

THE BEST-PAID PLANS

Some employers offer a single health insurance plan, while others allow you to choose among a number of different plans.

Whether or not you have a choice, employer provided health insurance is one of the best deals you'll find. Some employers pay most or all of the

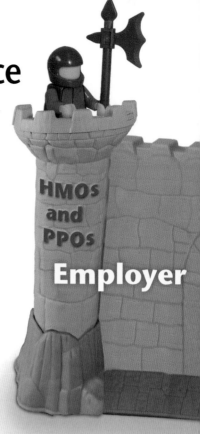

premium, or cost, that insurance companies charge, and many give you the option of paying for coverage for your spouse, dependents, or partner.

And because it's a **group plan**, even if you have to pay the full cost of your own coverage, you'll pay a much lower premium than you would if you were buying insurance as an individual.

SORTING OUT THE DETAILS

If you've never had to deal with health insurance, or if the details are a little blurry, it helps to recognize the basic differences between **managed care** and **fee-for-service coverage**.

Joining a managed care plan, which includes **health maintenance organizations (HMOs)** and **preferred provider organizations (PPOs)**, has its benefits—and its drawbacks.

The biggest advantage is cost. You pay a relatively low fee, called a **copayment,** for each visit to a participating doctor and each prescription you have

INSURANCE COST

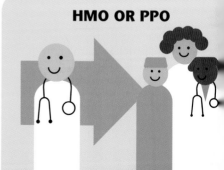

HMO OR PPO

Health Insurance

COBRA

If you leave a job for any reason, you may qualify to continue the health insurance your employer has provided.

The **Consolidated Omnibus Budget Reconciliation Act (COBRA)** of 1985 requires the insurer to offer you coverage for up to 18 months, or 29 months if you're disabled.

If you're used to your employer picking up most or all of your premium, COBRA will give you quite a bite. You're suddenly responsible for the full cost, plus up to 2% in administrative fees. But if you want to keep the same level of coverage you've had, chances are COBRA will be a lot cheaper than buying insurance on your own. And holding onto it until you take a new job or buy other coverage eliminates the risk of finding yourself without insurance when you need it.

filled. The cost is usually from $5 to $20, depending on the plan. Approved hospital stays are paid for.

The biggest drawback may be lack of flexibility. You must choose a **primary care physician** who is part of the organization to handle your basic care. That physician, sometimes described as a **gatekeeper**, refers you to **specialists** outside his or her area of expertise if you need additional care. In most cases, you must have a referral to see a specialist, and those referrals must be to doctors who also participate in the plan.

If you see a nonparticipating doctor, the visit may not be covered. And if your primary care physician doesn't feel you need a referral, you may have to pay the cost of a visit yourself.

Fee-for-service coverage, also known as **conventional health insurance**, works the opposite way. You can visit any physician you want, but you've got to pay all of your medical bills up to a predetermined **deductible**, usually around $250. After you reach that level, you can submit claims for your costs, and your insurance company will reimburse you, usually for about 80% of the cost they approve for the treatment you've had. That may be 80% of what you spent, but it's typically less.

FEE-FOR-SERVICE

Tricks of the Trade

You can avoid nasty surprises if you know how things work.

TO YOUR HEALTH

If you're self-employed, don't have a job, or your employer doesn't provide healthcare insurance, there are still ways to find affordable coverage. Many college alumni associations offer plans to recent grads, and professional associations and other organizations sometimes offer affordable group plans that are as reasonably priced as an employer's plan.

If you don't have access to any of these options, it's sometimes possible to be covered under a parent, spouse, or partner's plan. And of course, you can buy an **individual policy**, although you'll pay a considerably larger premium. You'll probably also have to pass a physical to qualify, which can be a roadblock if you have serious health problems.

If saving money on healthcare costs is more important to you than having a way to pay for everyday care, you might want to consider a **major medical only plan**. The high deductible brings down your premium, so you'll be able to protect yourself from major medical expenses without spending lots of money.

But be aware of what you're getting into by adopting this strategy. If you end up having a lot of small- or medium-level medical costs, your checkbook may need even more care than you do. This type of insurance doesn't usually kick in until you've spent $2,000 or sometimes more.

STOCK PLANS

Some employers offer **employee stock ownership plans (ESOPs)**. An ESOP is a trust to which the company contributes shares of newly issued stock, stock the company owns, or the money to buy stock. The shares go into individual accounts set up for employees who meet the plan's eligibility requirements.

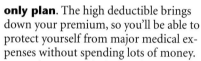

An ESOP can be part of a 401(k) plan or separate from it. If it's linked, your employer may match your contributions to the plan by adding shares to your ESOP instead of cash to your investment account. The one drawback is that a large percentage of your total retirement portfolio may be in a single investment—your employer's stock. That can make it harder to keep your account diversified, though it's not a good reason to turn down the opportunity to participate in the plan.

A BAD WAY TO SAVE

You might be tempted to have too much of your salary withheld deliberately so you'll get a substantial refund when you file your tax return. Getting the check might feel good and might justify a vacation or give you the down payment on a car. But think about it this way: Uncle Sam has had free use of your money for up to 15 months. And you get back only the amount you put in.

If you're afraid you won't save regularly on your own if you have a chance to spend the money first, ask your employer about having a certain percentage deposited directly into an investment or savings account. That way, the money has the potential to grow.

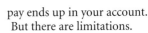

If you leave your job, you have the right to sell your shares on the open market if you work for a publicly held company or back to the ESOP at fair market value if you work for a privately held company.

WORTH WAITING FOR

Each employer sponsored retirement plan may have slightly different rules about how you qualify to participate.

At some jobs, you can start contributing with the first paycheck you receive. At others, you sometimes have to complete a waiting period, sometimes as long as a year, to be eligible. Once the year is up, you may also have to wait for the next **enrollment date**, such as the beginning of each quarter or twice during the year. In the meantime, you can be putting the money you'd contribute to the plan into an IRA.

If you're changing jobs and want to roll over the assets from your former job, ask if the waiting period must apply. Some plans are more flexible than others and have a shorter waiting period for rollover assets. If you have to wait, you can open a rollover IRA for your old plan assets and contribute to a traditional or Roth IRA during the waiting period.

BORROWING FROM YOUR PLAN

You may be able to borrow against the assets you've accumulated in your employer sponsored retirement plan. You generally have to repay the principal plus interest within five years.

There are some advantages to borrowing from your plan. There's no credit check, there's usually no delay in arranging the loan, and the interest you

pay ends up in your account. But there are limitations.

The amount you can borrow is capped, so you may not be able to access enough money to meet your needs. You may have to pay a substantial fee to arrange the loan. And you rarely earn as much from interest you pay back as you would if your account value was fully invested.

A potentially larger problem looms if you leave your job for any reason during the term of the loan. You'll probably have to repay the full amount within 30 to 90 days of your departure. If you don't, you're in default and the remaining loan balance is considered a withdrawal, subject to income taxes and early withdrawal penalty.

MY PLAN

CHANGING YOUR WITHHOLDING

If you start making more money, should you change your withholding? The answer depends on whether anything else is changing in your life.

If you're starting a second job—especially a freelance one where taxes aren't withheld by your employer—you may want to increase withholding at your first job to cover the taxes you'll pay on this new income stream. Or if your marital status changes—say, if you get married and move and take a higher-paying job—you'll want to update your W-4. But if you're just making more at the same job, the amount of money you're having withheld will increase proportionally to your new salary, so you don't need to adjust anything.

Credit: Convenience with a Caution

Credit is handy, but it has some risks.

As you become financially independent, credit is likely to play a bigger and more important part in your economic life than it has before.

There's a lot that credit can do for you. If you need money—especially in an emergency—and you don't have the cash on hand, the immediate buying power of a credit card can be a lifesaver. And through longer-term arrangements like car loans and mortgages, credit makes it possible to pay for things you wouldn't otherwise be able to afford.

But there is another side to the story. Credit makes spending money easy—sometimes too easy. So you can get into credit trouble by spending more than you can easily repay.

THE BIG PAYBACK

The flip side of the buying power that credit gives you is that you've got to pay back the money you spend. As obvious as this might seem, it can be surprisingly easy to forget how much you've charged when it seems like you have free money at your fingertips.

In return for the privilege of using credit, you're required to pay a **finance charge**. For credit cards, this means that **interest**, which is calculated as a percentage of the amount you owe, accumulates on any unpaid balance.

GIVE YOURSELF A LITTLE CREDIT

If you don't have a lot of cash, being able to buy things on credit can be a big help when you're furnishing an apartment or buying clothes to wear to work.

Using credit can also make your daily life a lot easier. Most merchants require a credit card number to reserve a hotel room, an airline flight, or a car rental, and of course, having a credit card is a prerequisite for shopping by phone and over the Internet.

Credit also allows you to get the most out of your money over time by taking advantage of the classic "buy now, pay later" philosophy. The most basic—and probably the most common—example is the **cash float** that credit cards provide. A cash float is the time between when you buy something with credit and when you pay the card issuer for that item.

For example, say you use a credit card to buy a compact disc online on October 10, and you receive a bill from your card company on November 5 that's due November 25. If you mail in a check to pay the bill on November 20, the check doesn't clear your bank until November 27, almost seven weeks after you spent the money.

CREDIT IS AS CREDIT DOES

You're probably already familiar with using credit. If you don't have a credit card in your own name—and most college students and recent graduates have at least one—you may have used a card linked to your parents' account.

And even if you haven't used a credit card or taken a loan, you've probably dealt with lots of transactions that work the same way.

 Many meal plans and cards in school dining halls allow you to get food on a daily basis and pay for what you've spent at the end of the semester or year.

 The CD and video clubs you see in magazines give you a large number of discs or tapes at essentially no cost based on the agreement that you'll purchase full-priced items in the future.

Magazine subscriptions that offer "pay later" options agree to send you the magazines you want and let you pay later.

For loans, the finance charge usually includes fees for the cost of arranging the credit, as well as the interest expense.

The problem with finance charges is that you can end up paying considerably more than your purchase originally cost. And while many credit cards don't impose a finance charge if you pay back the credit you've used within a certain period of time, most loans and some cards start charging from the moment you start spending.

Each credit arrangement has its own particular features, but one thing is true in every case: The longer you take to pay back what you've spent, the more using credit will cost. Interest can build up amazingly quickly, especially on big balances. And if you miss payments, you run the risk of having to pay late fees—at $25 or more a pop—and even ending up with a bad credit rating, which can make it difficult to get credit later on.

Here's a tip: Don't live off your credit cards. If you've lost your job or the job hunt isn't going well, it's better to take a loan from your parents than to charge your living expenses.

—Jeanette V., 27

Of course, you don't want to get overly aggressive. If you try to stretch the float to the limit, your payment may be late. That could cost you a late fee on top of a finance charge.

By allowing you to buy large items now while taking years to pay off the full price, credit arrangements like mortgages and car loans use this cash float principal on a larger scale. Only in this case, the float is known as **leverage**, or using a small amount of your own money to buy something of much greater value.

How Credit Works

You've got to go in circles if you want to go places with credit.

Using credit is a snap. You buy a jacket or pay for dinner by simply handing over a credit card and signing a receipt. And then you don't have to pay the bill for several weeks, and you may be able to spread your payment over months—or even years.

But you want to be sure the way you're using credit is better for you than it is for the credit provider.

WHO'S WHO?

Buying on credit is a process that involves three parties: you, the seller you're buying goods or services from, and your **creditor**, the bank or other institution that puts up the money to make your purchase possible. When you sign a **credit agreement**—or sometimes simply provide your credit card number—you agree that the creditor will pay the bill for your purchase, and you'll pay back the money.

The merchant you buy from also pays the creditor a fee, usually a percentage of the purchase price. Part of the cost of doing business is making it easy for people to buy—and that's what credit does.

WHAT'S WHAT?

When you get a credit card, you're arranging to use what's known as **revolving credit**. That means you have repeated access to a limited supply of money, known as your **credit limit**. As you charge purchases, you use up

1 Credit is the fuel that propels you through transactions and purchases. When you start a credit relationship, it's like having a full tank of gas to go where you want.

Credit Tank

4 But if you refill your credit line by paying back what you've used, you'll be back at the beginning of the credit cycle and ready to get rolling again.

part of that credit limit. But as soon as you repay any part of what you've used, you're free to use the amount again without having to reapply.

For example, if your credit limit on your credit card is $1,000, and you charge $400, you've still got $600 to use. And if you repay the $400 at the end of the month without charging additional purchases, your credit limit is back up to $1,000 again.

BORROWER BEWARE

If your credit card bill invites you to skip a month's payment without penalty, the lender isn't doing you a favor. If you take the offer, you probably won't owe a late fee, but you will owe finance charges on your unpaid balance. And any purchases you make after the due date you skipped will probably accumulate interest from the day you make them.

THE PRINCIPAL IDEAS

In return for using borrowed money, called the **principal**, for longer than a few weeks—or from the time you spend the money until payment is due—you agree to pay the creditor a finance charge. For credit cards, this really means the interest that accumulates on any unpaid balance, calculated as a percentage of the amount you owe. Other charges, like annual fees for the use of the card, or fees for paying late or exceeding your limit, are extra.

In most cases when you're considering a credit agreement, you won't be able to negotiate better terms with a

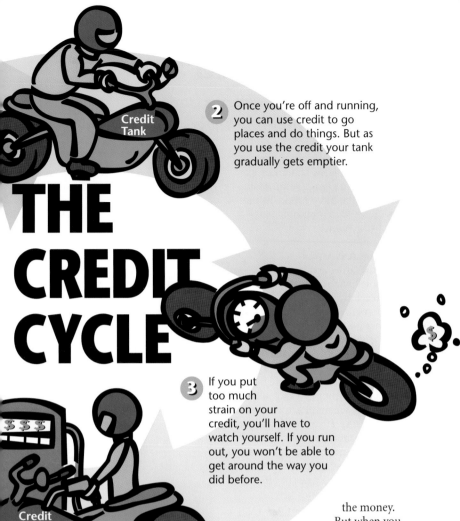

THE CREDIT CYCLE

2 Once you're off and running, you can use credit to go places and do things. But as you use the credit your tank gradually gets emptier.

3 If you put too much strain on your credit, you'll have to watch yourself. If you run out, you won't be able to get around the way you did before.

creditor than whatever the standard offer is at the time. But that doesn't mean you can't find a good deal. Whenever you're in the market for credit, doing some serious comparison shopping may help you find a lower interest rate, smaller fees, or some other way to save money.

VARIATIONS ON THE THEME
A **line of credit** is another type of revolving credit. Banks and other credit providers sometimes offer customers a line of credit to make it convenient for them to borrow larger amounts than they might be able to put on a credit card.

Often, when you have a line of credit, you get a pack of special checks that look just like regular checks. In fact, you use them the same way as conventional checks, and can write them for amounts up to the credit limit your lender sets. The difference is that you'll get a bill, including finance charges, for spending

the money. But when you repay, you can use the amount again.

You might also have a line of credit that gives you **overdraft privileges** on your checking account. If you do, your bank will cover checks you write, up to your credit limit, if you don't have enough money in your account to cover the amount of the check. You pay interest on amounts transferred from your line of credit, but you can use the line over and over if you need it.

CASH ADVANCES
As useful as credit cards can be, there are times when you need cash. If you don't have the money you need in your bank account, most credit cards allow you to get **cash advances** at ATMs. The only thing you have to do ahead of time is arrange for a personal identification number (PIN), just as you do with an ATM card.

With most cash advance arrangements, you start owing interest from the moment you get the cash. And that interest may be charged at a higher rate than you pay on your regular card purchases.

Getting Carded

Recognizing differences among cards can help you pick the right one out of the lineup.

It's hard to miss the obvious differences among the small plastic rectangles in your wallet. But it's equally important to understand the more subtle distinctions among the types of cards that are available.

WHAT'S IN A NAME?

Classic credit cards, with names like Visa, MasterCard, Discover, and American Express Blue, let you charge purchases up to your **credit limit**, a specific dollar amount that may be increased over time.

You have to pay back at least a minimum amount of your outstanding balance every month—though, of course, you can always pay more than the minimum. If you pay less, you'll find an underpayment penalty tacked onto your balance. If you don't pay the minimum for several months, the fees will mount and interest charges continue to build. Before long, your borrowing privileges will probably be cut off.

DEBIT CARDS: AN ALTERNATIVE

If you want to have the convenience of a credit card without as great a potential for debt problems, consider a **debit card**. Many banks offer debit cards, usually as a feature of your checking account. And they're accepted just about everywhere credit cards are. They let you pay for purchases directly with money that's withdrawn from your checking account.

A debit card doesn't guarantee you won't overspend, especially if you have overdraft protection on your account. But at least your bank balance will be obvious the next time you visit an ATM or check your account online. That makes it harder to deceive yourself about where you stand financially at any given moment.

And while having your debit card rejected for insufficient funds could be embarrassing, it can also be a good wake-up call.

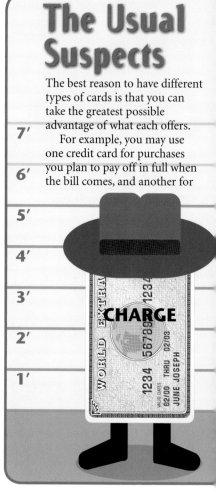

The Usual Suspects

The best reason to have different types of cards is that you can take the greatest possible advantage of what each offers.

For example, you may use one credit card for purchases you plan to pay off in full when the bill comes, and another for

Though they work like credit cards when you make a purchase, American Express, Diners Club, and Carte Blanche aren't actually credit cards at all, but **charge cards**. Their main attraction—in addition to what some users feel is a prestige factor—is that they don't have an official credit limit (though you may run into a situation where a large charge isn't approved).

The potential downside of these cards is that you have to pay off whatever you spend each month. If you don't, you're likely to incur a finance charge. And you may find your account frozen so that you're unable to use your card, especially if you don't respond to a reminder that your account is overdue.

Each company has its own policy for handling delinquent accounts, so it pays

purchases, especially large ones, you plan to pay off over time. That's one way to avoid interest on day-to-day charges while you're financing a big-ticket item.

Similarly, you might use a debit card to avoid having to carry cash, saving

your credit or charge card for more expensive purchases. Or you might use a charge card for your regular expenses and a credit card for larger purchases so you can stretch these payments over time.

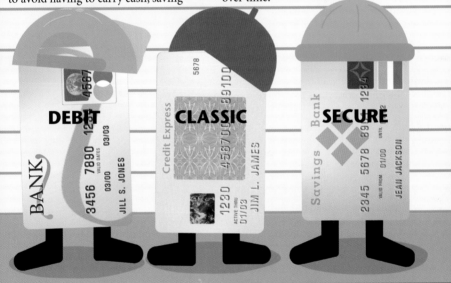

to know the consequences of being late. You don't want to be inconvenienced or embarrassed by being unable to pay for a purchase, or charge a meal, because your card privileges have been revoked.

A SECURE START

If you're just starting to use credit—or if you're trying to recover from past credit problems—a **secured credit card** can help. You use the card just as you would a regular card, and there's nothing to identify it as a secured card to retailers or others who accept it. But the card is backed by a savings account at the bank that issues the card.

You can charge up to the amount you have in that account (or less if you choose a lower credit limit). You'll owe interest just as you would on a regular

card, but the money in your account guarantees your ability to make every payment. The account also earns interest, which may help offset the interest you'll owe on outstanding balances.

If you use the card and repay regularly, you should qualify for a regular credit card. If the bank doesn't offer that upgrade after six months of regular repayments, you can ask when you will qualify.

But be wary of scams and shady deals if you've had credit problems. Steer clear of any offer that:

- Promises to get you credit regardless of your history, especially for an up-front fee
- Requires you to call a 1-900 or other pay-per-call number
- Says that it can guarantee to repair your credit history

It's in the Cards

Picking the credit card that's right for you can mean the difference between being fortunate and owing a fortune.

HOW MUCH INTEREST

18% APR
1.5% a month

AVERAGE DAILY BALANCE

Balance of $2,000

If you pay $1,000

% PAY

Previous balance	$2,000
Amount paid	−$1,000
New balance	$1,000
Interest due on	$1,500
Monthly APR	x 1.5%
Amount you owe	$22.50

It's not hard to find a credit card. Actually, you'll probably get so many card offers that the hard part will be choosing the one that's best for you. The adult card market is pretty much saturated, and studies have shown that people become very loyal to the first card they get. So card companies do everything they can to sign up younger customers.

Even if you're sure you won't let yourself become tied to one card for life, it's still crucial to find the card that's right for your needs from the start. That means thinking about how you'll use a card and what elements of credit are the most important to you.

PICK A CARD...BUT NOT ANY CARD

If you know you'll pay your bill in full every month, you've got a fairly easy choice. Since you won't have to worry about what interest will cost you, look first for a card with a **grace period**, ideally one that's 25 to 30 days long.

SAVING GRACE

If you've got a 25-day grace period, does that mean your payment is due on noon of the 25th day or at the end of the day? Or the beginning of the 26th day? Or the end of it? And in what time zone? Many card companies print this information on every monthly statement, but if yours doesn't, make sure you ask.

These questions might seem like splitting hairs, but knowing exactly when the money is due can be the difference between making an on-time payment or owing interest and late fees you shouldn't be paying.

A grace period is the time between when your bill is calculated and when you have to pay the amount that's due. With a grace period, interest doesn't start accumulating on charges until after the payment due date. There's a catch though. It can take several days to get your bill after it's been calculated, and several days for your payment to reach your creditor. The grace period clock is ticking that whole time. So the longer the grace period, the more time you have to pay, and the better the chance you'll get your payment in on time and avoid finance charges.

If you can find a card with a long grace period and no **annual fee**, that's an added plus. It means you can get all of the benefits of credit at none of the cost.

OUT OF GRACE

Of course, you may not pay off your bill every month. Most people don't. In fact, the average person under 35 owes $2,700 in credit card debt. If you're likely to pay

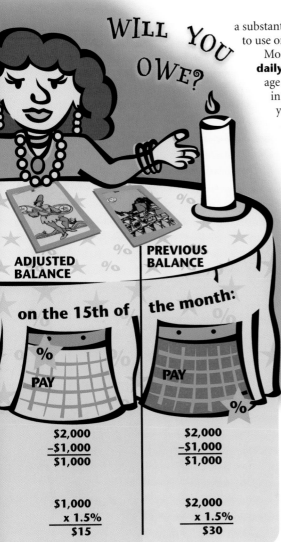

WILL YOU OWE?

ADJUSTED BALANCE

PREVIOUS BALANCE

on the 15th of the month:

PAY	**PAY**

ADJUSTED BALANCE	PREVIOUS BALANCE
$2,000	$2,000
−$1,000	−$1,000
$1,000	$1,000
$1,000	$2,000
x 1.5%	x 1.5%
$15	$30

a substantial effect on what it costs you to use one card rather than another. Most cards use your **average daily balance**, which is the average of what you owed each day in the billing period to figure your interest. So, for example, say you had a previous balance of $2,000 on the card with an 18% APR, and you pay $1,000 on day 15 of a 30-day period. You'd owe a total of $22.50 ([$2,000 x 1.5% x 15 days + $1,000 x 1.5% x 15 days] ÷ 30 = $22.50). Under this method, you'll save money by paying off a large amount of your balance during the billing cycle.

The **adjusted balance** method is the cheapest of all. The card company subtracts whatever payment you make from your beginning balance and charges interest based only on the remaining amount. So if you paid off $1,000 of a $2,000 bill, you'd pay interest on just the remaining $1,000. That would only cost you $15.

But if the lender charges interest based on your **previous balance**, payments you make during the month don't reduce that balance. Instead, you have to pay interest based on the full amount you owed at the start of the period, making it the most expensive method—you'd owe $30 ($2,000 x 1.5%) in this case.

only part of what you owe each month, the grace period becomes insignificant since you'll never get the benefit of it. Anytime you have an unpaid balance after your statement's due date, interest accumulates on all of your purchases, even the new ones.

What matters most in this case is the **interest rate**, or finance charge. The higher the rate, the more using credit will cost you.

A FEW POINTS OF INTEREST

The biggest factor in what any card costs is its **annual percentage rate (APR)**. For example, if your card has an APR of 18%, you'll pay 1.5% interest on your balance every month. That means if you owe $1,000, you'll have $15 added to your bill. That may seem like a small amount, but what if you're only paying the minimum amount each month, probably $15 or $20? You'll barely be making a dent in your balance.

Pay attention to the way a card company calculates interest, too. It can have

DON'T BELIEVE THE HYPE

When you don't have a lot of money or credit, all of the offers pouring into your mailbox—and into your email inbox over the Web—can be very seductive. Try to resist the urge to sign up with the card that has the flashiest package, or promises perks you don't need. Instead, focus on the fine print: Every card is required by law to include a **disclosure box** somewhere in its promotional materials. There you'll find the information you need on interest rates, annual fees, and the other important elements of a card agreement. So if the rate in huge type on the front of the envelope looks too low to be true, check the disclosure box to find out the real story.

Stacking the Deck

When you're auditioning credit cards, you've got to deal with a cast of thousands.

A credit card can be more than just a way to buy things without having to pay cash. But the extra bells and whistles that many credit cards offer rarely come for free. And they're not all worth what you have to pay for them, either. So you've got to ask yourself two questions: What credit card perks—if any—do you need? And are they worth your money?

AFFINITY CARDS: SUPERCARDS?

Some banks offer credit cards that are cosponsored by another organization, perhaps an airline, an ecommerce site, your college or university, or a charity. These **affinity cards** give you something extra on top of the usual credit privileges: You can earn frequent flier miles, get special deals, or make contributions when you use the card.

Affinity cards are becoming more and more common, so chances are you'll be able to find one that does what you're looking for. And if you plan to accumulate a lot of charges on your card—say, if you use it for business—these cards can be a great way to save money or support organizations or causes that matter to you.

Next!

But do the math before you sign up for an affinity card. Rewards tend to accumulate slowly. For example, at the rate of one frequent flier mile for every dollar you spend, an average card can require as much as $40,000 in charges to earn a single round-trip ticket. And affinity cards may have higher than average annual fees, so if you're not going to use your card for most of your purchases, you might end up paying more than you're actually getting back.

PRECIOUS METALS

Your first credit card is likely to be a classic card. And if you get an American Express charge card, it's likely to be green. But you may be offered gold, platinum, or titanium versions—each charging a higher annual fee than the basic card.

If you're wondering whether it makes sense to spring for the added cost, the answer depends on whether you'll use the additional benefits enough to justify the price you'll pay.

For example, if a platinum card costs several hundred dollars but gives you membership privileges at two or three airlines' club facilities, it

CREDIT CARD AUDITIONS

Audition for Precious Metals

might be worth it if you travel on those airlines. The same is true if the card covers car rental collision insurance and you rent cars frequently.

But if you pay the extra charge expecting to get better service from the merchants where you use the luxury model card, you're likely to be disappointed.

TEASERS AND TRANSFERS

Lots of cards offer **introductory rates**, also known as **teaser rates**, to attract new customers. For example, you might find a card with a 3.6% interest rate for the first three months, before it increases to a more typical 13% to 15%.

These offers can be a mixed blessing. On one hand, if you know you're going to run up a balance, it might save you some money to have a low rate at first. And if you know you can pay off your balance in a few months, you may be able to take real advantage of the teaser rate.

But if you're not watching the calendar, it's easy to let your teaser time run out. At that point, you may start accumulating more serious interest—often at a higher rate than you could find on a card without a teaser rate. And while switching cards every few months to take advantage of teaser offers might save you money, it can

make you seem unreliable to creditors in the future.

Many cards will also offer you the chance to transfer balances from other cards to their card at a lower rate than your usual rate. This can be a convenient way to consolidate your debt, and may save you money. Just be sure you know the date you'll have to pay off the balances you transfer before the actual higher rate kicks in. And be sure to find out ahead of time what all of the charges will be.

A LITTLE PROTECTION

Some cards—including most charge cards, but also more upscale versions of credit cards—offer various kinds of protection on the purchases you make with the card. For instance, a card might provide collision insurance on a car rental so that you don't have to pay extra for that coverage, or automatically protect things you purchase against damage or theft up to a certain value. These features can save you money and provide peace of mind, but be sure that you'll get some use out of them if you're going to be paying fees for them.

CASH WITHDRAWALS

When you get cash using a credit card and your PIN, you're borrowing against a cash advance limit. But if you have an American Express card and you're part of their Express Cash program, you can use your card to withdraw money directly from your checking account for a flat fee of 3% of your withdrawal.

Since you're not borrowing, there's no finance charge. And there's no fee for signing up for Express Cash. But the annual fee for the card is higher than on most classic credit cards.

Audition for EXTRAS

Plastic: Power or Peril?

If you don't have enough green when you charge, you'll end up seeing red.

Being smart about credit involves more than just picking the right card. You can be diligent about choosing a card with no annual fee, a long grace period, and the lowest APR on the market, and still run up thousands of dollars of debt.

What can really get you into trouble with credit cards is how much you charge, or more precisely, how much more you charge than you're able to pay off. Whether or not you stay ahead of the credit game depends on how you handle some all-too-familiar situations.

MONEY DOWN...AND OUT

A lot of credit card spending is done on the spur of the moment, when you haven't planned on buying something and you don't have cash on hand.

For example, suppose you're out for dinner or drinks with a group of friends and the server brings one check? It makes life a lot easier just to pull out your card and collect cash from everyone else—to say nothing of the ego trip it can be. But chances are you'll put the cash you collect into your pocket rather than your bank account. And it's equally likely that one or more of the group says they'll have to owe you their share.

Of course, if you've got the will power to set aside the cash you get from your friends until your monthly bill comes due—or the brain power to keep a running tally of how much the laggards still owe you—there's nothing wrong with picking up the bill once in a while. But if it gets to be a habit, or if your friends take advantage, it can turn into a real problem.

IT'S NO BARGAIN

One of the best uses of credit—the ability to buy things at a good price even if you don't have the cash—can also create a financial nightmare if you do it too often.

For example, what if there's a huge sale at a store where you've had your eye on a new piece of electronic equipment, or a new jacket, or something as essential as a bed? There's no question that getting 40%—or whatever—off the full price is a good deal.

But if that extra $500 or $900 on top of your typical credit card balance is more than you can repay, you may be digging yourself into a hole. And the more often you add a major purchase, the larger, or deeper, the problem can get.

PAY ONLY THE MINIMUM EACH MONTH

OPEN AN ACCOUNT TODAY AND SAVE 10%

SLOW

DANGER IN STORE

Often, when you're shopping at a retail chain or department store, you'll be offered a chance to apply for a store credit card, usually with an opportunity to save money on your current purchase or to take advantage of other savings in the future. This can seem like a good deal when you're standing at the checkout counter, and it can even *be* a good deal sometimes. But don't forget what it will mean for you down the line.

First of all, these cards often have even higher APRs than regular cards, sometimes as high as 25%. Some have shorter grace periods than regular cards. And it's a fact o life that people tend to spend more using a card than they do if they're spending cash. The lure of the additional 10% or 15% savings the store offers you to open and use your account can tempt you into spending more than you might otherwise.

In addition, taking on multiple cards—and their credit limits—can make you look like a risk to future creditors. You can appear to be overextended even if you stop using the cards after taking advantage of the initial offer. Surprisingly, canceling the cards you're not using doesn't necessarily improve your credit standing.

And while it may seem inconsequential, the more bills that arrive during the month, the harder it can be to stay on top of all of them, even if the total amount you charge isn't huge.

THE BARE MINIMUM LEAVES YOU EXPOSED

What you charge each month becomes all too clear when your monthly statement arrives, and you see how much you owe. There are basically two ways to deal with your statement: You can pay all or at least a substantial portion of your balance. Or you can make the minimum payment, which must be enough to pay all of the interest and some principal each month.

While paying the minimum keeps you out of trouble with creditors, it's much more costly in the long run, since you'll always be paying interest on a large amount, which doesn't decrease very rapidly. For example, if you pay a minimum balance of $20 on a $300 purchase you made with a card that has an 18% APR, you won't pay off that debt for 18 months, and it'll end up costing you $343—over 14% more than the purchase price. And that's if you don't buy anything else in the meantime.

But if you could pay $50 a month, it would take you only seven months to repay and cost $317 in total. Of course, if you paid off the whole $300 when you first got the bill, it wouldn't cost you anything extra—that's the best possible credit scenario.

I worked for six months as a personal assistant to a film executive. As part of my job, I had to go shopping for my boss. I charged big-ticket items to my own personal credit card—cases of champagne, expensive clothing, a $500 gift for the executive's fiancé—and then waited to get reimbursed. My credit limit doubled while I had the job, and when the executive was late in reimbursing me, I had to pay the interest that accumulated on the balance.

—Caddie H., 24

Your Monthly Statement

Your monthly credit card statement tells you what you owe—and a lot more.

The monthly billing statement your credit card company sends you provides the most important things you need to know about your credit account: how much you owe and when payment is due.

But you can find out a lot more, including all the activity in the account since your last statement, and what you're paying in fees and finance charges, if anything.

AN EYE TO THE STATEMENT

Every credit card statement looks a little bit different, but they all contain pretty much the same information. Make sure you understand everything that's being reported—it's the key to using your card wisely.

It's always a good idea to check over each entry to make sure that every charge is accurate, and that every payment you make shows up for the right amount. It's easy for a merchant to slip up and charge you twice for a purchase,

Your **credit limit**, also known as your credit line, shows the total amount of credit you have access to with your card.

Charges are the purchases and cash withdrawals you make. Each of these has a date and a reference code in case you need to discuss it with your card company.

Credits are amounts subtracted from the balance you owe because of payments you've made, corrections of incorrect charges, or merchandise you returned.

Your **previous balance** is the amount you owed when your last statement was issued. Your new balance is calculated using this number as a starting point.

Your **finance charge** is the interest that has accumulated on the balance you owe.

Your **total available credit** is the amount you could still charge at the time that the statement was issued. It's equal to your total credit limit minus any charges that were outstanding at the time.

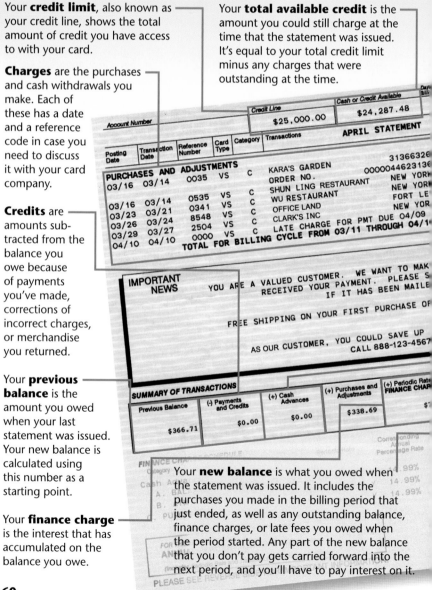

Your **new balance** is what you owed when the statement was issued. It includes the purchases you made in the billing period that just ended, as well as any outstanding balance, finance charges, or late fees you owed when the period started. Any part of the new balance that you don't pay gets carried forward into the next period, and you'll have to pay interest on it.

or forget to credit you for something you return. And credit card numbers can easily be stolen, leading to charges that aren't even yours to begin with.

Paying close attention to your statement can also help you evaluate your spending habits and improve them if you want to. Since you can see exactly where your money goes, as well as how much you spend, it's easy to figure out what portion of your card spending is going to discretionary items and what portion is going to necessities.

ONLINE STATEMENTS

Many card companies let you view your statement online. This can make the information you'll find a lot more timely and convenient, as well as a lot more useful. You can check your account status any time and from anywhere. But that's just the beginning.

Since online records are updated regularly, you can see exactly what's happening with your account whenever you want, without having to wait for a paper statement to arrive once a month. And most cards let you make payments online, which can save you time and make your life a lot easier.

Some cards even go beyond a simple online statement—they can notify you by email when a billing period on your account closes, for example, or when a payment posts to your account. If your card offers extra reminders like these, it can't hurt to take advantage of them.

Your **statement closing** or **billing date** shows the date your statement was created. Any charges and payments on your account after this date will appear on your next statement.

The **minimum payment due** is the amount you have to pay in order to keep your account in good standing—that is, without incurring any penalties or harm to your credit history. This amount must cover the interest and some principal.

You have to pay at least your minimum payment by the **payment due date** or you'll be penalized with additional charges or late fees.

You can use your credit card to withdraw money from an ATM up to your **cash advance limit**. You pay a finance charge from the day you withdraw until the amount is repaid. There's usually no grace period on cash advances.

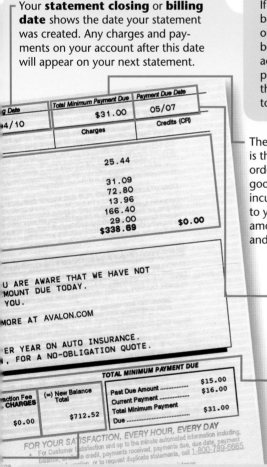

g Date	Total Minimum Payment Due	Payment Due Date
4/10	$31.00	05/07

Charges	Credits (CR)
25.44	
31.09	
72.80	
13.96	
166.40	
29.00	$0.00
$338.69	

U ARE AWARE THAT WE HAVE NOT
MOUNT DUE TODAY.
YOU.

MORE AT AVALON.COM

ER YEAR ON AUTO INSURANCE.
. FOR A NO-OBLIGATION QUOTE.

TOTAL MINIMUM PAYMENT DUE

action Fee .CHARGES	(=) New Balance Total		
		Past Due Amount	$15.00
		Current Payment	$16.00
$0.00	$712.52	Total Minimum Payment Due	$31.00

FOR YOUR SATISFACTION, EVERY HOUR, EVERY DAY
For Customer satisfaction and up to the minute automated information including,
balance, available credit, payments received, payments due, due date, payment
information, or to request duplicate statements, call 1-800-789-6685.

Building a Credit History

You start laying the foundation of your credit history the first time you borrow.

There's a vast—and constantly growing—amount of information about how consumers use credit. And you can be sure that when you apply for credit, whether it's as routine as asking for a new credit card or as significant as applying for a mortgage, potential creditors will check out your credit history.

MAKING HISTORY

The three major national **credit bureaus**—Equifax, Experian, and TransUnion—collect two types of information about you. The first is how you use credit, from how much you owe on car loans, mortgages, and credit cards to the timeliness of your monthly payments. There's an incredible amount of data that falls into this category—about two billion items a month, which breaks down to an average of 11 items per credit user.

Credit bureaus also store public information about you that might influence the way lenders evaluate your creditworthiness. This can include anything from records of bankruptcies and foreclosures to court judgments and divorce proceedings. But credit bureaus don't gather any personal information that isn't directly credit-related, such as how much you make, what you spend on rent or utilities, or anything you pay for in cash.

Credit bureaus make the information they've collected available—at a price—to creditors, banks, potential employers, landlords, and others who have a legal right to evaluate you based on your use of credit. Most information remains on your report for quite a while. Damaging activity can appear for up to seven years even if the account is closed or inactive. And bankruptcies can stay on your report for up to ten years unless the state where you live imposes a shorter limit.

WHO'S KEEPING SCORE?

Did you ever wonder why it takes a retail store or an online credit card company just a minute or two to approve your application for credit? Did you know that you may be quoted one interest rate on a car loan while the next person to apply is offered a higher—or lower—rate? These kinds of things happen because credit decisions often come down to the **credit score**, or **FICO® score**, you're assigned by the credit bureau your potential creditor contacts.

All credit bureaus use a process called credit scoring, or credit modeling, to evaluate the risk you pose to a potential creditor. According to Fair, Isaac and Company, the firm that developed the software the bureaus use to do the calculation, the score depends on five main criteria:

- Your payment history, and specifically whether you pay on time
- The total amount you owe
- The length of your credit history
- The amount of new credit you have
- The types of credit you use

Creditworthy behavior in these categories works in your favor, while risky behavior works against you. And while there are general standards for the way the criteria are applied, there are no

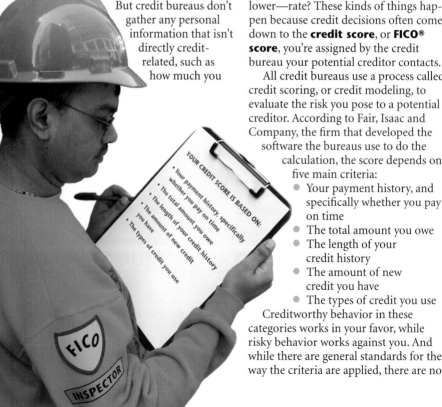

YOUR CREDIT SCORE IS BASED ON:
- Your payment history, specifically whether you pay on time
- The total amount you owe
- The length of your credit history
- The amount of new credit you have
- The types of credit you use

FICO
INSPECTOR

fixed rules. Credit bureaus aren't required to explain the way they arrived at your particular score, and you shouldn't expect them to do so. All they are required to provide are up to four reasons for the score, which the lender must tell you if you ask why your application was denied.

WHAT'S THE SCORE?

When you get a FICO credit score, you're going for a high number. The top 20% of reports that are evaluated get scores over 780, while the lowest 20% get scores under 620.

Each lender sets its own standard for what qualifies as an acceptable score, and determines the interest rate for which you qualify based on your score. The best rates—in this case, the lowest, or **prime rates**—go to applicants with the highest scores. Applicants with low scores, sometimes called **sub-prime borrowers**, may be offered credit at higher rates.

Credit scoring has its advocates and its detractors. Those in favor say that, in addition to the advantage of speed, lenders get a better picture of your creditworthiness with this timely snapshot. That, they say, makes the system fairer. Critics argue that reducing all the information about you to a single score can provide a distorted picture. They also say that a lender can find it easier to say no on the basis of what appears to be a value-neutral system.

WHAT THE LENDER KNOWS

Lenders may go beyond your credit score in evaluating your application. For example, they may want to know the amount you earn, whether you've been at the same job for two years or more, and if you've lived at the same address for a while. In addition, lenders may be more willing to grant you credit if you already have banking or investment accounts with them.

GOOD NEWS AND BAD

Building a good credit history means developing good credit habits:

- Get a credit card and use it responsibly
- Make purchases every billing period, and pay them off in full and on time
- Apply gradually for additional credit

At the same time your potential creditors are looking for evidence that you've used credit wisely, they're also alert to danger signs. Those red flags can include:

- A large number of open credit accounts, especially if they have large credit limits
- Three or more payments more than 30 days late
- Loans in default

Reading a Credit Report

If you can read credit reports, you'll know what they're saying about you.

If you can think of anything that might reflect badly on how creditworthy you are, chances are it's already in your credit report. From new credit cards you haven't used yet to more substantial issues, like a repossessed car or unpaid college loan, credit reports cover a breadth and depth of information that can be staggering—and somewhat alarming.

The trick is to be sure that creditors will like what they see when they check your report. The good news is that you can improve your chances of getting approved if you review your report ahead of time. That way you'll have time to correct any mistakes and clear up any outstanding problems with payment histories.

A general rule of thumb is that the more credit you're planning to apply for, the sooner you should take a look at your report. If you want to rent an apartment or get a new credit card, check just before you apply to make sure the information on your report doesn't cause any unnecessary delays. If you're applying for a mortgage, give yourself at least three to six months to sort out any problems and put your best foot forward.

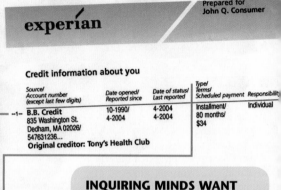

Credit information about you

Prepared for
John Q. Consumer

experian

Source/ Account number (except last few digits)	Date opened/ Reported since	Date of status/ Last reported	Type/ Terms/ Scheduled payment	Responsibility
–1– B.B. Credit 835 Washington St. Dedham, MA 02026/ 547631236... Original creditor: Tony's Health Club	10-1990/ 4-2004	4-2004 4-2004	Installment/ 80 months/ $34	Individual
–2– America's Be PO Box 7871 S Ft. Lauderdale, 547632536...				:ibil ith ons
–3– America's B 547638896...				ized

Each of your credit **accounts** is listed on your report, along with the credit issuer's address and your account number. Any accounts that could have a negative effect on your credit history show up at the top of your report, with dashes before and after their identifying numbers.

Type and terms show whether an account is revolving credit or an installment loan.

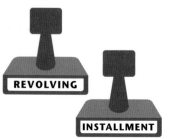

REVOLVING

INSTALLMENT

INQUIRING MINDS WANT TO KNOW

Your credit report also contains one or more lists of creditors who've made inquiries about you or asked to see your report in the past 24 months.

That's important because potential lenders sometimes interpret repeated inquiries as evidence that you're taking on too much debt and overextending your ability to pay. And they may be reluctant to give you credit if you've already been rejected by other lenders. It does seem like a catch-22 that you've got to have a credit history to be able to get credit, but it's a fact of life.

There's a list of inquiries that won't hurt your credit chances. That's the list showing the creditors who want to offer you credit—including the unsolicited credit card applications you get in the mail. You can see that list, but it isn't released to other creditors.

Your **credit limit** is the most you can owe on an account. Your **high balance** is the most you've ever owed.

Comments

The **comments** section is crucial for evaluating your credit. It shows the status of the account, if you've ever paid a bill 30 days or more past its due date, and if so, how late. It should also show any comments you've sent to the creditor, such as noting that you've closed an account or disagreed with a charge or penalty.

The **most recent balance** is the amount you owed on an account as of your most recent statement.

Your use of credit gives a detailed payment history of each account, usually going back up to 24 months. It shows each monthly balance for revolving credit and the outstanding balance on installment loans.

eport date
ay 1
eport number   Questions?
3456-173634738   Call 888 397 3742   Page 1 of 4

credit limit or original amount/ high balance	Most recent balance	Comments
8,500/ 8,500	$1,321 as of 4-2004	Status: collection/past due 90 days. $548 past due as of 6-2004. Account past due: Collection as of 9-2003 thru 6-2004; 90 days as of 7-2004; ...days as of 11-2003, 6-1-2004, 6-29-2004; ...0 other times.

Your use of credit
The information listed below provides additional detail about your accounts, showing up to... ...ance history and your credit limit or original loan amount. Not all balance history information... ...Experian, so some of your accounts may not appear. Balance history information missing from... ...is indicated by a dash (—).

Source/Account number	Date	Balance	Date	Balance
America's Best Bank 547632536...	4-2004	35,100	12-2004	35,300
	3-2004	35,200	11-2004	35,400
	—	—	10-2004	35,500
			9-2004	35,600
America's Best Bank 547638896...	4-2004	0	12-2004	0
Between 2-1997 and 1-1998, your credit limit was $5,000.	3-2004	0	11-2004	0
	2-2004	0	10-2004	0
Between 8-1996 and 1-1997, your credit limit was $2,000.	—	—	9-2004	0

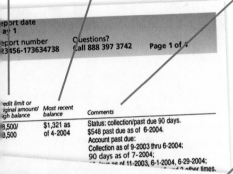

GETTING A REPORT

Everyone is entitled to a free credit report from each of the national credit reporting companies each year, thanks to the FACT Act. You can ask for all three at once or one every four months, either online at www.annualcreditreport.com or by calling 877-322-8228. Spreading out your requests is probably smart, so you'll know quickly if there's a problem. You're also entitled to a free report if you've been denied credit, employment, or insurance within the last 60 days.

You can request a report by phone or over the Internet. Contact Equifax at 800-685-1111 or www.equifax.com, Experian at 888-397-3742 or www.experian.com, and TransUnion at 800-888-4213 or www.transunion.com.

TO THE LIMIT

If you've never had a card before, chances are the credit limit you're offered will be pretty low to start. But as you use a card, the company will probably increase the amount it will allow you to charge. And once you've got one or two cards, you'll find yourself getting card offers with higher and higher limits. That's because your use of the credit identifies you as someone companies can trust to spend money—which means you can probably make money for them.

Credit card companies don't offer you higher credit limits as rewards for good behavior, or because having access to more money is always in your best interest. That's why you don't have to waste any energy worrying that a card issuer might cut off your credit, or cancel your card, because you owe them money. In fact, as long as you don't **default**, or stop paying what you owe, the more you owe them, the happier they'll be. That's exactly why they go looking for your business in the first place.

Dealing with Credit Problems

You might find yourself invaded by problems with creditors and credit. But you've got rights to help you sort things out.

With almost 200 million consumers in the credit-reporting system, mistakes are inevitable and problems are sure to crop up. Stolen cards, lost payments, billing errors, and disputes with lenders can all cause you grief as well as harm your potential for getting credit in the future. But as long as you know your rights and take a few precautions, it's not hard to take action if problems come up.

Your first step should be a preventative one. Hold on to all of your credit-related information and paperwork, including receipts from purchases you make using credit cards, billing statements, canceled checks used to pay credit bills, credit agreements, and policy changes, and anything and everything else that seems important. That way you'll have evidence to back you up in case of any disputes.

TRUTH, LENDING, AND THE AMERICAN WAY

When you apply for credit, you're protected against discrimination under the **Equal Credit Opportunity Act (ECOA)**. The ECOA states that lenders cannot reject credit applicants on the basis of race, sex, marital status, age, national origin, or the fact that you receive government assistance. In fact, they're required to consider public assistance in the same light as other forms of income.

You're also protected in any credit agreement by the **Truth-in-Lending Act**, also known as **Regulation Z**. Under Regulation Z, lenders have to tell you in writing certain terms of the credit they're offering before you borrow from them.

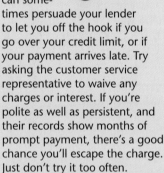

ASK NICELY

Please?

If you're usually an exemplary credit customer, you can sometimes persuade your lender to let you off the hook if you go over your credit limit, or if your payment arrives late. Try asking the customer service representative to waive any charges or interest. If you're polite as well as persistent, and their records show months of prompt payment, there's a good chance you'll escape the charge. Just don't try it too often.

It's even possible to talk a creditor out of raising your APR. There's often no reason for these increases other than the issuer's desire to make more money. Politely pointing out your history as a good customer may get them to back off.

REGULATION Z

FAIR CREDIT REPORTING ACT

FAIR BILLING

FITTING THE BILL

If you find what seems like an error in a credit billing statement, you're entitled to dispute it under the **Fair Credit Billing Act**. This law defines billing errors as:

- Charges that you, or other people authorized to use your account, didn't make
- Incorrect credits or payments, or ones that show the wrong amount or date
- Charges for items that you didn't accept on delivery, or that weren't delivered as agreed upon
- Computational errors
- Failure to deliver your billing statement to your current address with 20 days notice of an address change

DOING YOUR PART

If you receive a statement you believe to be incorrect, you have 60 days from when it was mailed to notify the creditor in writing. Be sure to write to the address for billing inquiries, and to include your name and account number as well as an explanation of which portion of your bill you think is incorrect.

The company then has 30 days to acknowledge your letter, and 90 days to resolve the problem. During this time you are free to use the card, and while you should pay all parts of your bill that aren't in dispute, you don't have to pay the disputed amount, or any finance charges that it incurs.

Some creditors are quick to respond to queries and complaints, while others may stall, insist you're the one in error, or otherwise make your life difficult. If you're involved in a long-term credit relationship, as you might be with a mortgage or car loan, you may just have to be persistent and patient.

But since you have such a choice of credit cards, there's no reason not to cancel your account if you find that your card company seems unwilling to respond to your inquiries or slow to get them resolved. But even if you cancel a card, you'll still have to resolve all outstanding issues and payments.

REJECTIONS AND REPORTS

If you're denied credit, you're entitled to know why. So contact the lender. There's always the possibility that the decision was based on incorrect or inaccurate information. One study found that 29% of all credit reports contain errors that could result in your being denied credit. Another pegged it at 33%. As simple a mistake as misspelling your name can mean your credit history gets mixed up with someone else's.

If you've been turned down, the lender has to tell you which credit report contains the damaging information. Ask the credit bureau for a copy of your report—it's free if you ask within 60 days of being rejected. If you find that your report does contain an error, notify the credit bureau that issued it and the lender that rejected you immediately. The **Fair Credit Reporting Act** requires that they both investigate your dispute—although they're not required to make any changes to your report if they don't think the change is warranted.

Check your report again 90 days after you contact the credit bureau and lender. If it hasn't been changed as a result of your complaint, you're entitled to write an explanatory comment of 100 words or less that must be included in all future reports.

FREEZE!

Once you dispute a credit billing issue, the creditor you're dealing with can't release potentially damaging information about that charge to other creditors or credit reporting companies.

Getting in Step with a Loan

Loans can be tough to get when you're young. But a strong credit history can keep you in contention.

If you want to do something that costs a lot of money, like starting your own business or making improvements to your home, you'll probably need a loan to help pay for it. The process of applying for, obtaining, and repaying a loan—sometimes described as **installment credit**—isn't easy, especially when you're just starting out. Unlike credit card issuers, lenders won't be beating down your door to offer you loans. But there are things you can do to make it easier to get a loan—and to pay it off.

APPLYING YOURSELF

When you apply for a loan, you're judged on many of the same criteria that are used when you apply for a credit card, including your credit score and whether you have a regular job. But since there's often a lot more money at stake with a loan, you'll probably find lenders digging deeper into your financial situation.

For example, a lender may ask to see current paystubs or recent income tax returns as evidence of what you earn. But having a bigger income doesn't automatically make you eligible for a loan. How you handle the income is equally important.

In deciding whether you'll be able to repay the loan, lenders also look at your **net worth**. That's the value of the things you own, including cash,

Assets
– Liabilities
= Net Worth

securities, and personal property, minus what you owe on your credit cards or other debts. Lenders will probably ask you to provide this information on a standard form. And they typically ask for the account numbers and balances for whatever bank, brokerage firm, and credit card accounts you have.

Being judged on your net worth can work against you when you're young. After all, you probably don't own that much in terms of assets or property, which is why you're applying for the loan in the first place. But if you're investing for retirement with a 401(k) or you've opened an IRA—which you should be doing anyway—the money you've invested can help strengthen your financial position. While lenders can't dip into your retirement accounts to cover your loans, they usually include the amounts as part of your assets. That should give your application a boost.

WHAT A LOAN COSTS

When you're shopping for a loan, check the total cost. While the **principal**, or the amount you borrow, and the **interest** you pay are very important, you've got to look at other factors as well. The **term** of the loan, and the **fees** you pay for applying and for having your credit checked are also crucial.

A loan's **annual percentage rate (APR)** helps you compare costs because the APR takes into account the fees you pay to arrange the loan, as well as the annual interest charges. That gives you an accurate picture of what you'll actually pay to borrow.

Interest rates, and therefore APRs, vary widely, and are significantly lower in some periods than others. A drop or increase in rates reflects what's happening in the economy as a whole, and whether borrowing overall is relatively cheap or quite expensive. What doesn't change, whatever the rates are, is that you want the lowest APR you can find.

Of course, on a $10,000 loan that you'll repay over three or four years, it doesn't work out to a very big difference in your monthly payments. But if you ever take a mortgage, where you'll be paying many tens (or hundreds) of thousands of dollars over 30 years, an extra 0.35% or 0.50% means you'll be paying a lot more money.

Lenders are required by law to tell you a loan's APR in their advertising, which means you can compare different loans on equal terms without having to do any of the figuring on your own.

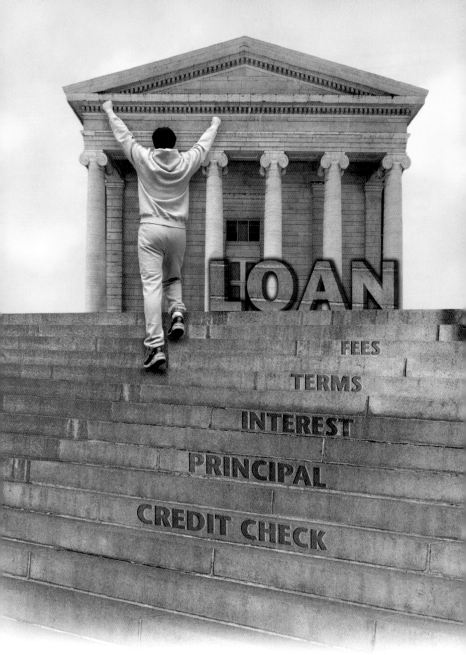

BORROWED TIME

The term of a loan is an important factor in keeping your cost as low as possible. While a shorter term means that you'll be making fewer, but larger payments, it also means that you'll be paying interest for fewer years. That brings your total cost down. So $10,000 you borrow at 10% would cost you $322.68 per month on a three-year loan, $253.63 on a four-year loan, and $212.48 on a five-year loan. But the total cost with the three-year loan would be about $11,590—instead of more than $12,700 after five years.

FIRST THINGS FIRST

When you start paying back a loan, every check you write pays off a certain portion of the interest and a certain portion of the principal. Banks and most other commercial lenders **front-load** their interest so that they can maximize their profit. Since you're paying mostly interest at first, it takes a substantial amount of time to begin reducing your principal.

> **Amortization** is another word for the process of paying off a long-term loan. It comes from the French verb for "to bring to death." Although you might feel like you're the one dying after a few years of payments, it's the loan that's being amortized.

Repaying Student Loans

If you're on the ball, you can plan your repayment strategy.

Half of all college graduates have a student loan to repay. For most, it's probably the first big, long-term debt they've had. So if the lingering cost of your education is causing you a little bit of panic, you're not alone.

Adjusting to the fact that you have thousands of dollars to pay back when you're just starting a career can seem like an impossible burden. Fortunately, it's not. There are a variety of ways to structure your payments, which can make student loans easier on your nerves as well as your pocketbook.

PICKING A PLAN

There are several ways to repay government-backed **Stafford Loans**. Each one fits a slightly different financial situation, so you need to think seriously about what you can afford when you pick a repayment plan.

Remember that the best plan for you isn't necessarily the one with the lowest monthly payments—or the one with the highest payments, for that matter. Think about what you can afford now, and what you can reasonably expect to pay down the road.

And you're not making an irrevocable decision. You can always switch plans if you need to.

The **standard repayment plan** requires you to make fixed payments of at least $50 a month for a set period of time. The time repayment takes depends on how much you've borrowed, but it won't be more than ten years. This plan will probably let you pay back your loan quickest, and cost you the least overall, provided you have the money to keep up with the payments.

The **extended repayment plan**, like the standard plan, requires fixed payments for a set period. And while your payments are still at least $50 a month, they're usually significantly less than what you'd pay using the standard plan. That's because your payments are stretched over a considerably longer period, anywhere from 10 to 30 years. Of course, this increases

the overall interest you'll pay over time, but it can make your payments a little more manageable.

If you're not making a lot of money right now, but you're expecting to have a higher income in the future, the **graduated repayment plan** might be the best plan for you. Your payments are stretched out over 10 to 30 years as with the extended plan, but there is an added cushion because your payments start out smaller. The minimum monthly payment could be less than $50 and increases every two years.

Standard
Fixed payments, fixed term

Extended
Lower payments, longer term

Graduated
Increasing payments over time

Income-Contingent
Varying payments for up to 25 years

The **income-sensitive repayment plan**, which applies to private lender loans, adjusts your monthly payments annually, based on your income and student loan debt. The repayment period lasts up to ten years.

The **income-contingent repayment plan** sets your monthly payments based on your income, which can give you some security if you have a volatile cash flow. What you pay each year rises or falls based on what you make, and there's no set minimum payment. You can take up to 25 years to repay under this plan. After that, any amount that's still unpaid will be **discharged**, or canceled, by the government, although you'll have to pay income taxes on the amount that's forgiven.

HOLD ONTO THAT DEBT!

If you're not used to having debt, you might find yourself wanting to pay off your student loan as quickly as possible. But as crazy as it seems, it can actually be a good idea to pay off your debt on a long-term schedule.

That's because for many people, the interest charges are tax deductible. So if you've got extra cash you could use to repay the loans faster, it may make better sense to put the money into savings and investments instead. That may be especially true of money you put into a tax-deferred savings plan, such as an IRA or 401(k).

DEFERMENT, FORBEARANCE, AND DISCHARGE

If something happens that makes it hard for you to pay back your student loans, you may be able to postpone payment for a set period of time. You can apply to **defer** your loans, for example, if you're in school at least half time, if you take a parental leave from work, or if you enter a public service organization, such as the armed forces or the Peace Corps. Unemployment, temporary disability, and other events that may keep you from earning money can also make you eligible for deferment. If your loans are deferred, your payments stop, and the balance doesn't accumulate interest.

If you don't have a valid reason for deferment but you still can't pay your loans, you can request a **forbearance**. If a forbearance is granted, you won't have to make payments, but your loans will continue to accumulate interest.

In certain very special cases, it's possible to have your loans **discharged**, or canceled altogether. This usually requires an extreme circumstance, such as total disability. The government sometimes also discharges loans as a reward for working full-time in particular positions with the disabled or low-income families, or in law enforcement, teaching, or other public service areas.

KEEPING UP ONLINE

If you want to get the latest information about your Stafford Loans, from finding out the current interest rate to calculating total costs, you'll find useful resources at www.ed.gov/DirectLoan. Or call 800-848-0979 to speak with someone directly.

HANDLING OTHER LOANS

If you've taken several loans to pay for your education, keeping track of what you owe and making your payments on time can be an even greater challenge. That's because the term, repayment schedule, and lender may vary for each loan.

One solution may be to consider **serialization** or **consolidation**.

With serialization—if you qualify—you arrange to make the payments on a number of different loans to a single address. The loans themselves aren't affected. With consolidation, you take a new loan, the consolidator pays off your existing loans, and you make just one payment.

Ask your financial aid office for more details.

Paying for Graduate School

If you study the different ways to pay for grad school, you can probably swing it.

Graduate school can be a huge step. It's likely to mean a dramatic change in your lifestyle, both personally and financially.

And while getting a postgraduate degree often means you'll make more money down the road, you'll still need to finance your education while you're in school.

If you depended on financial aid to pay for college, you'll be familiar with some of the procedures. But you'll find some new things to deal with as well.

DO THE FAFSA FIRST

Regardless of your financial situation, your first step should be to fill out the **Free Application for Federal Student Aid (FAFSA)**. It determines your eligibility for federal **Stafford Loans**, as well as many grants, scholarships, and other non-federal aid. Filling out the FAFSA can be incredibly time-consuming, and you're asked all sorts of personal financial information, so be sure to leave yourself enough time.

The federal deadline is June 30 of the year for which you'll need funding, but the sooner you get your application in, the better chance you'll have of getting federal money. Most graduate programs require that you submit your FAFSA in early spring for their financial aid programs. You can complete the application online at www.fafsa.ed.gov if you want to save a little paperwork.

If you encountered the FAFSA when you applied for undergraduate aid, you'll find this one welcome change: You aren't required to report your parents' income or assets. So you won't lose the chance to get federal money because of your family's financial situation.

FEDERAL AID

Stafford Loans are the most common form of federal aid—in fact, most graduate students are eligible to receive them. And since they can provide as much as $18,500 a year, and up to $138,500 in total, with an interest rate that was 3.37% in 2004-2005, it's a good thing they're so widely available.

There are two kinds of Stafford Loans. **Subsidized** loans require that you demonstrate financial need. If you're in school at least half time, or if your loans are in the grace period or in defer-ment, the government pays the interest on them. You can take **unsubsidized** loans regardless of your financial situation, but you'll be responsible for all of the interest that accumulates.

Based on your income, you may also be eligible to take a **Lifetime Learning Credit** when you file your federal income tax return, reducing the amount you owe.

EARN WHILE YOU LEARN

Assistantships are another way to finance graduate education. The opportunities they provide for research or teaching can enrich your resume as well as your bank account.

Assistantships are almost always competitive positions, and they can often cover a substantial part of your tuition and living expenses—in recent years, full-time students with assistant-ships have earned an average of $8,700 a year. And that's money you're earning, not borrowing, so there's no payback or interest later on. (You do owe federal income tax on fellowship income, but not on scholarship aid.)

But make no mistake about it—you'll be working to earn that money. Many assistants work 20 hours a week or more, especially those in teaching positions. That kind of time commitment can be difficult when you're already busy with your own work, and it can make what you're getting paid seem a lot smaller.

In recent years teaching assistants at some schools have unionized to petition for better working conditions. If you're consider-ing applying for this combination of work and aid, make sure the schools and departments you're looking at treat their assistants fairly.

SOME STRINGS ATTACHED

Your employer may agree to pay for part or all of your education. But this free schooling isn't exactly free. Typically, you've got to agree to go back to your job for at least a few years after you get your degree.

If you've been happy at the company, and you want to stay in the same line of work, this can be a great deal. But be sure it's really what you're looking for. You don't want to get locked into a job or career path that looks a lot less exciting at the end of grad school than it did at the beginning. And pulling out of an agreement with your employer can result in penalties and fees, as well as education costs you weren't expecting.

If you want to take advantage of an employer's offer without committing to something you're unsure of, see if you can work out an agreement that lets you go to school part-time and still work. That way you can keep your hands in both worlds without making a future commitment you may later regret.

WHO GETS WHAT?

Students in different graduate programs often finance their educations in different ways. While students in PhD programs can often get assistantships and grants as well as loans, medical and law students usually can't work while in school and depend more heavily on loans.

But it always pays to ask what's available. A state university might offer you a reduction to in-state tuition rates even if your home is elsewhere. Or a private university may have discretionary funds it can make available to select students.

If more than one school seems interested in you, you may be able to negotiate more help from the one you prefer by mentioning what another school is offering you.

Dealing with Debt

It's dangerously easy to fall into debt when you're young.

You're probably making more money now than you ever have before. But you've probably got more expenses too. That's a dangerous combination. It's far too easy to spend a lot more than you actually have. And that leads to trouble with debt.

Of course, getting sick, losing your job, and other things beyond your control can also land you in debt. But there are usually ways to prevent debt problems, as well as ways to improve your situation if you do get into trouble.

WARNING SIGNS

The best way to handle debt is to avoid it. Spending within your means and watching how you use credit—especially credit cards—can help. But if you don't know what debt trouble looks like, it can sneak up on you. If you find yourself in any of these situations, it's time to start managing your finances more carefully:

- Regularly paying only the minimum on your credit cards or missing payments altogether
- Regularly hitting your credit limit on your credit cards
- Needing to withdraw money from your savings account to cover bills or basic expenses
- Having trouble paying for an unexpected expense, such as car repairs
- Depending on unpredictable income, such as overtime pay or money from a second job, to get by

FINDING REMEDIES

To start dealing with debt, take a close look at your monthly spending and pinpoint some areas where you can cut back to free up more money for your debts. Then make paying your bills every month a priority—not an afterthought.

CAN YOUR CARDS

Since interest on credit cards is higher than on most other sources of credit, they're particularly dangerous if you're teetering on the brink of debt disaster. If you find yourself in such a situation, it might be time to get rid of your cards, especially if you've had problems with overspending. Even if you keep one card for emergencies, it's probably smart to pay in cash or with a debit card whenever you possibly can. That way you can keep a closer eye on where you stand financially.

GET OUT OF DEBT

If you end up in serious debt trouble, don't give up. You can take a number of approaches to resolving debt problems, a process often known as **restructuring** debt.

The simplest thing you can do is to ask your creditors to rewrite the terms of your credit agreements so that your bills are easier for you to pay off. This often means smaller payments over a longer period of time, which of course means you'll end up paying more interest and increasing your overall cost. But that's usually a better deal in the long run than having to default or declare bankruptcy.

If you need help dealing with your creditors or figuring out the best way to handle your debts, a **non-profit credit counseling service** can help. For a relatively modest cost, they'll help you

BANKRUPTCY

Filing for **bankruptcy** is a last resort, something you should be considering only if you're looking at an extremely long period of debt repayment, usually five or more years. When you file for bankruptcy, the court where you file allows you to **discharge** your debts. Under such a plan, you pay less than the full amount you owe, and your lenders recover some of their money.

By resolving your debt, bankruptcy allows you to get a new start. You're legally protected from creditors, so you know that your situation can't worsen. But bankruptcy damages your credit history, and you stand to lose many of your assets in order to repay your debts.

Remember, too, that bankruptcy doesn't wipe out amounts you owe the government for income taxes or student loans, or get rid of any alimony obligations you may have.

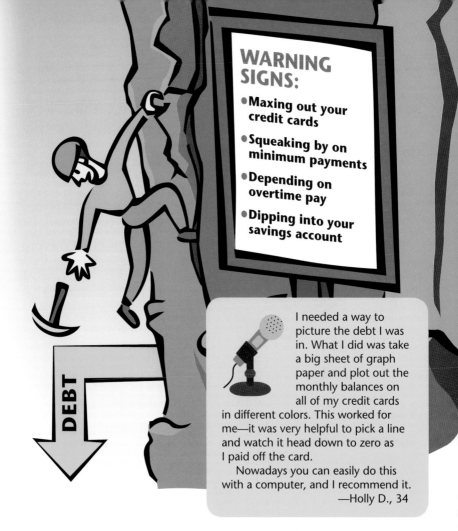

I needed a way to picture the debt I was in. What I did was take a big sheet of graph paper and plot out the monthly balances on all of my credit cards in different colors. This worked for me—it was very helpful to pick a line and watch it head down to zero as I paid off the card.

Nowadays you can easily do this with a computer, and I recommend it.
—Holly D., 34

come up with a repayment plan that's feasible for you. Check out:

- The National Foundation for Consumer Credit at 800-388-2227 or www.nfcc.org

Credit counseling is really about changing the way you handle money, not just getting out of a financial tight spot. A repayment plan is a great idea, but you also want help creating a spending plan and advice on how to stick to it. Otherwise, history is apt to repeat itself.

PUTTING IT TOGETHER
Using a **loan consolidator** is another way to handle debt. Consolidators lend you money to pay off your bills, and you repay the consolidator instead of your original lenders.

While debt consolidation may allow you to make a lower, more manageable monthly payment, the interest rates and fees that consolidators charge can be much higher than you'd otherwise pay. And since many of them impose heavy penalties for paying off your debt ahead of schedule, you might find yourself stuck with even more financial headaches than you had before.

STUDENT LOAN DEFAULT
There's a slightly different course of events if you fall behind on repaying student loans. If you don't make a payment on time, you're considered **delinquent** (although chances are you won't have too much trouble if you're only a day or two late). If you don't make any payments for 270 days, your loans go into **default**. The consequences can vary, from a damaged credit rating to having your federal tax refund withheld or even having your wages **garnished**.

If you're subject to garnishment, a percentage of your paycheck is withheld to pay your loans. Since that means your employer will find out about your situation, it can be embarrassing and potentially damaging to your job security as well as financially harmful. Default can also result in your having to pay any costs your lender incurs in order to collect the outstanding money you owe. It's smart to contact your lender to try to put together a feasible plan before you get into real trouble.

Points of Interest

Whether you're watching out for pitfalls or on the lookout for good deals, the more you know about credit, the better.

KEEP YOUR CARD COVERED

Various companies offer credit card transaction recorders that slip over your card and fit easily into your wallet. These little envelopes let you keep track of what you've charged on your card just as you do with your checkbook ledger, which can make the size of your monthly bill a lot less of a surprise. To obtain one, visit www.ucms.com/news.html or ask your card issuer if it provides them.

TO WHOSE CREDIT?

If you're married or have a partner, you can apply for credit as an individual or make a joint application. The advantage of applying jointly is that both incomes and job histories count, which may help you to qualify more easily. The drawback is that both of you are responsible for paying the bills no matter which of you spent the money. This can be a problem if you have different spending habits, or if your relationship comes to a bad end.

Most financial advisers urge you to keep at least one card in your own name or apply for credit as an individual, even if your other finances are handled jointly. And they suggest using the card regularly and paying the bills on time. This way, if you suddenly need access to credit in your own name, you'll have it.

What won't help you build a credit history is being listed as an authorized user on someone else's individual account. Even if the card you're using has your name on it, your use of credit won't be recorded in your name. It will go on the record of the main cardholder.

REASONABLE USE

If you're not charging more than you can pay off, there's no reason not to put as many expenses as you want on your credit card. It saves you the trouble of having to carry cash and simplifies your monthly bill-paying. And, if you have an affinity card, using it regularly is a good way to accumulate points for air travel or make contributions to your favorite charity.

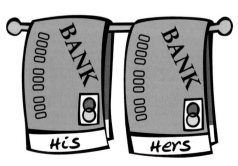

SECURED vs. UNSECURED

Most loans you'll qualify for are secured loans. That means you are required to put up assets as collateral on the money you borrow. If you can't repay your debt, the lender can **repossess**, or take back, your collateral and sell it to recover what you owe.

For example, a car loan is a secured loan—if you don't make your payments,

the lender has the right to repossess your car. The same goes for a mortgage, with your house as collateral.

Unsecured loans don't require collateral, just your promise to repay—and the lender's belief that you're creditworthy. For example, your student loans are unsecured, though if your parents took a home equity loan to help pay your tuition, it's secured by the family home.

Because unsecured loans carry a greater risk, commercial lenders may be reluctant to make them if you need the money for anything but educational expenses. The lenders who regularly make unsecured loans tend to charge high interest rates.

You'll probably have an easier time arranging an unsecured loan informally, from a friend or family member.

SWEETENING THE DEAL

The government offers several incentives for doing the right thing with your student loans. For example, if you sign up for electronic debiting for your monthly payments, you'll get 0.25% deducted from your interest rate—in addition to the time and energy you'll save by not having to send a payment by regular mail each month. And you may get an interest reduction for having a good record of on-time payments. Check the Direct Loan website regularly at www.ed.gov/DirectLoan or with your lender for information about these offers, and be sure to take advantage of them whenever you can.

TAX-SAVING TIP

Another thing that makes student loans a good kind of debt is that you're often eligible to deduct the loan interest you pay on your federal tax return. You're likely to qualify for the deduction as long as your modified adjusted gross income (MAGI) is $65,000 or less—or $130,000 if you're married and file a joint return—and the loan wasn't from a relative or employer. Your loan provider will send you IRS Form 1098-E, "Student Loan Interest Statement," to report how much interest you've paid. Check out IRS Publication 970, "Tax Benefits for Higher Education," for more information.

THE BASICS ON BASIS POINTS

If you're looking for a loan (or dealing with repaying one), you'll probably hear lenders mention **basis points**. They're referring to the unit that's used to measure differences in interest rates.

A basis point is 1/100 of a percentage point. So if you're paying 7.25% interest on an adjustable rate loan, and the rate goes up 25 basis points, your new rate is 7.5%.

1 BASIS POINT = 0.01%

25 BASIS POINTS = 0.25%

Get Real (Estate)

"Getting your own place" can mean anything from renting the roof over your head to making a substantial investment.

How happy you are with where you live—the physical space, the ambience of the neighborhood, the proximity to your job, even the price you pay—can have a major impact on your attitude toward all the other parts of your life: your job, your friendships, even your relationship with your family. That probably means that finding the right place to live becomes one of your priorities, even if it's a continuing process of trial and error.

Everybody's housing wish list is a little different. If you work long hours, you might value an easy commute to your job. If reducing your living costs or increasing your living space is more important than convenience, you might decide to live farther away—though you need to factor in the cost and the time of your commute. If you're single, you might also think about living with your parents for a while until you can afford a place where you'd really like to live.

SHOULD YOU BUY?

For many young people, the cost and obligation of a mortgage are too intimidating, so they rent. But if you're at the right point in life and the price is right, buying a home can be a smart idea. For example, if you're starting a family, taking a long-term job, or if you know you're going to be in one place for more than a few years, you might want to think about taking the plunge and investing in a home.

Owning your home can often be a way to get more space for less money. And there can be some real financial advantages. While you'll have to keep up with a mortgage and regular property taxes, you can deduct these taxes, as well as interest on your mortgage, on your tax return. And in a good economy with a strong real estate market, your home can be a great investment.

Of course, those mortgage payments—and the down payment that you'll have to make up front—aren't exactly small, and not everybody has that kind of money to lay out in their first years on their own. And even if you do have the money, it's possible that buying

LOCATION, LOCATION, LOCATION

If you're like many young people, the kind of job you've got, or the kind you're looking for, will have a large effect on where you end up living. Of course, that's not the case for everyone—some people base their job searches around where they want to live. But whatever your priorities are, you don't have to be locked in by a decision. You've got a bunch of alternatives to consider, each with its strengths and weaknesses:

CITIES

SUBURBS

RURAL

isn't the smartest thing, at least not yet. If it's likely you'll move around in the next few years, a home can be a burden even if it is a long-term investment. And your money might earn more with less obligation elsewhere.

IS IT SMART TO RENT?

Having relatively little long-term obligation is one of the things that makes renting so appealing to young people. While you may have to come up with a few months' worth of rent as a deposit, it won't be as much as a down payment. You're not responsible, financially or otherwise, for repairs or maintenance. And since you haven't actually made an investment in your home, you can move without worrying too much about losing money.

But of course, not making that investment means that as long as you rent, you'll be spending money to live without getting anything back other than a roof over your head. And if prices skyrocket, chances are you'll

be at the mercy of the market. Still, the short-term affordability and the freedom to move make renting the more popular choice for young people.

Whatever you do, try to make a decision that makes sense financially and emotionally—don't pick a place you know you'll hate just to save money, or move somewhere you can't afford because it seems like a cool place to be.

MUSICAL HOMES

Chances are you'll move regularly in the next few years, changing your home as often as you change your job—or maybe more often. If you keep track of what's been good and what's been awful about the places you leave, you'll have a better sense of what to look for in your next house or apartment. For starters:

- Check water pressure in the shower and the age of the bathroom fixtures
- Consider the age of the stove and the state of the refrigerator
- Ask about laundry facilities
- Check the electric outlets and wiring

PROS	CONS
● Lots of other young people ● A wide variety of jobs ● Easy access to things to do and see	● High cost of living ● Less space and fewer amenities for your money
● Cheaper and larger housing ● Commuting distance to a city without having to live in it	● Costs and inconvenience of commuting ● Fewer young people ● Fewer local jobs
● The most space for your money ● Seclusion from the city	● A smaller selection of jobs ● Usually few young people ● Limited access to urban areas

Finding a Place to Rent

Picking the right house or apartment in a tight rental market can be like finding a needle in a haystack.

While renting requires less immediate cash and fewer obligations than owning a home, that doesn't mean that it's cheap or easy, or that it comes without strings attached. In fact, finding—and keeping—a good rental can be pretty difficult, especially if it's your first time. But if you know what you're getting into beforehand, you have a better chance of finding a good place at a good price.

BUDGET AHEAD

Before you start looking at places to rent, it helps to get a sense of the money you'll have to lay out. The real estate section of a local paper or the classifieds of a free weekly are good places to find the going rental rates. And there are websites for most major regions that can also give you good ballpark figures.

You'll probably find a fairly wide range of prices in most areas, so it's

natural to wonder how much you should be paying. After all, while rent will probably be your biggest single expense, you don't want to get locked into paying more than you can afford. In an ideal world, you wouldn't want to spend more than 25% to 30% of your take-home pay on housing, but in a lot of high-demand urban areas, you'll probably find yourself having to give up closer to 35% to 40%.

FINDING YOUR PLACE

Looking for a place to rent can be trying, especially when you've got limited time and money. In many places, opportunities come and go quickly. So you'll want to take advantage of ways to streamline the process. But do so wisely—some ways of finding housing are more expensive than others.

PAYING UP FRONT

Once you've got a good sense of what a month's rent will cost you, you can use that amount to start budgeting for how much you'll have to pay up front when you sign a lease. Exactly *what* you'll have to pay for depends on where you live, but most places will require at least the first and last months' rent. Often you'll have to pay an additional month as a security deposit. And if you use a broker, you could end up shelling out from 8% to 18% of a full year's rent.

Asking around among family, friends, and other people can't hurt. You can never tell who might know of something opening up that you can slide into easily without having to pay heavy fees. If you're working, see if your company

Get Professional Help

REALTY

Apartment Listings

WWW.

Search

has a bulletin board where coworkers might post sublets or leases you might be able to take over. College alumni clubs and websites are another great place to find these kinds of leads.

Searching the classifieds can sometimes be helpful, and the rental listings websites that exist for most larger areas can be a convenient way to see properties as well as read about them. The problem is that lots of other people use these resources too, so in most high-demand areas the listed properties will be gone before you find out about them. But these resources are a great way to find brokers in the areas you're interested in.

Using a broker can help you find a good place, especially if you're not familiar with the area. Brokers can provide great access to properties, and many even take you around from place to place. Just remember that they can be aggressive—and costly—salespeople. In some cities, landlords pay brokers' commissions, but elsewhere the cost is on the renters' shoulders.

Using listings services, which exist in many large urban areas, can be hit-or-miss. These companies sell listings of apartments being rented without brokers, so you can contact owners directly. Listings usually cost a few hundred dollars for a series of ongoing reports, which makes them like a low-cost broker. The only difference is that other people are getting the same listings as you are, so you can end up running into the same problems you do with newspapers and websites. If you decide to go with a listings service, make sure you have the time and the patience to get something out of it.

A New Lease on Life

Signing a lease can grant you independence—or imprison you in a bad situation.

No matter how much you're paying, your rent is likely to be a large portion of what you spend every month. So you want to know you're getting what you expect for your money. Part of that is making sure that you won't find any nasty surprises—like mice or a lack of hot water—in the place you're renting after you sign the **lease**.

But you have to pay close attention to the business end of things as well. That includes being aware of all the terms of your lease, and being sure you can live with them, before you sign.

CHECK YOURSELF OUT

While you should certainly look over your lease carefully, it's also important to remember that you're being checked out too. When you apply to rent a house or apartment, most landlords or brokers will check your credit history to make sure you've handled credit in the past in a way that suggests you'll make your rent payments consistently. You should also be prepared for your landlord or broker to pass on the cost of running the credit check, which can be as much as $50.

If you think your credit history might be a source of trouble, it's a good idea to request a free copy of your credit report beforehand at www.annualcreditreport. com. While you might not be able to erase any serious black marks on your record, you can identify and respond to any errors. Resolving them should help your chances of being approved for a lease.

If you are rejected because of credit issues, you have the legal right to know which credit bureau provided the

damaging information to the landlord or broker who rejected you, and that credit bureau is required to give you a free copy of the report in question. But it's up to you to figure out where the problems are and fix them before you apply again.

FINDING A GUARANTOR

Many brokers and landlords won't let you sign a lease alone if you're young or if it's your first rental, even if you have good credit and a high income. In these cases you need a **guarantor**, or **cosigner**, who agrees to pay your rent if you default.

The laws that govern guarantors vary from state to state. Some states require your guarantor to be a resident of the state where you're renting, while others allow guarantors from out of state. If you think you might need a guarantor, contact prospective brokers or landlords to find out the details *before* you start looking at and applying for properties.

OTHER REJECTIONS

You can be rejected even if you've got great credit. After all, there's always someone who might have a better or longer credit history, especially if you're fairly young and you haven't had a lot of experience with credit. In that case, there's not much you can do but try again with another place and keep up your good credit habits.

Cosigner

RENTAL AGREEMENTS

Make sure you know whether you're signing a lease or a **rental agreement**. They may sound like pretty much the same thing, and they do have similarities. But there are also some crucial differences you should be aware of.

The biggest one is how long they last. While most leases are for a year or two, rental agreements cover a much shorter period, usually 30 days. They're automatically renewed at the end of this period, unless either you or your landlord gives 30 days written notice.

Each of these has its own benefits and drawbacks, and the one that's best for you depends on your needs. If you know you will move within the year, a rental agreement might be a better idea. But in many cases your landlord can raise your rent on fairly short notice. Leases allow you to lock in your rent for at least a year, but if you move out before that year is up, you may well end up having to pay through the end of the lease.

Knowing the requirements can mean the difference between renting the place you want and getting turned down on a technicality.

LOOK BEFORE YOU LEASE

Your lease is a legally binding agreement between you and your landlord. Once you agree to it, you're obligated to keep to its terms, so be sure to read it thoroughly before you sign. The lease should include a few key pieces of information that ensure you're getting exactly what you're paying for:

- The names of all adults who will be living in the residence
- The exact property that's being rented (If it's an apartment, make sure the apartment number is listed.)
- The length of the lease and the dates it covers
- How much the rent is, when it has to be paid, and what the penalties are for late payment
- How much your security deposit is, and how it will be returned to you
- Which utilities are and are not included in the price of the rent
- The conditions for renewing your lease and for giving notice of your moving

If there are other rules that apply to the apartment—such as restrictions on pets, or rules about the use of facilities in the building—make sure that they're in the lease as well. And if the broker or landlord adds any handwritten terms to a standardized lease, make sure they're written in pen, initialed, and dated by him or her and by you and any other tenants.

Rules for Renting

Renting a home can be a walk on Easy Street—or a tug-of-war with your landlord.

You've got rights as a renter. Of course, your landlord has rights too. If all goes well during your tenancy, there's no reason that the two of you should butt heads. But if something goes wrong, you should know what the laws that govern your tenancy are—they can make your life a lot easier and help you come out on top financially.

HOME IMPROVEMENT

If you have the urge to make some improvements to your place, read the fine print of your lease before you jump into repainting the bedroom or tiling the bathroom. Many leases have clauses that prohibit you from making any alterations to the property, and disobeying this provision could cost you your security deposit at the very least.

If it costs your landlord more than that to undo the improvements you put in, you could end up in small claims court for the rest of the money. And while it's not likely to happen, your landlord is legally allowed to evict you for breaking the terms of the lease by altering the property.

Even if there's no explicit prohibition in your lease, it's probably a good idea to get your landlord's permission anyway, ideally in writing—and before you start. This way you'll have proof of permission if anything happens after the fact. And who knows? If your landlord thinks the work you're proposing to do is a good idea—one that might increase the rental's future value—you might even be able to deduct the costs from your rent.

Whether your landlord will make repairs on your apartment if you request them depends on what you're asking for—and on his or her attitude. While your landlord has to keep your residence in a habitable state, cosmetic repairs aren't required by law, so don't be surprised if your request for a new carpet or new fixtures falls on deaf ears. Of course if you have a good relationship with your landlord, or you can show a reason why the repair you want would be a good investment, you might get lucky.

THE MORE THINGS CHANGE

You're carrying on a long tradition when you start dealing with landlords. The relationship between landlords and tenants comes from the feudal system that existed in Europe between the tenth and thirteenth centuries.

Back then, rulers who owned land gave portions of it to lords, who would rent it to other people in return for military service or some of the profits from working the land. The rural tenants had no rights, and nowhere to go for better living conditions.

The landlords of nineteenth-century cities were equally autocratic, though in a vastly changed landscape of crowded tenements. They prospered by jamming as many people as possible into as small a space as possible—something that still defines city living.

Eventually, laws established minimal standards for plumbing and ventilation and required air space between buildings. One consequence was the push upward. Instead of five- or six-story walkups, metal-framed skyscrapers—a term first used to describe a tall building in 1891—changed the image of a landlord from hard-hearted individual to impersonal corporation.

The loose network of laws that establish your rights as a tenant

charged for part of what it costs your landlord to re-rent the property.

On the other hand, your landlord is obligated to find a new tenant as soon as possible, which means you hopefully won't have to pay out the rest of your lease. And some landlords will let you leave early if you pay a **termination fee** or give up your deposit rather than have to pay the rent every month. If you've got this opportunity, it could save you money, especially if you're not sure your landlord will be able—or willing—to re-rent your place right away.

It pays to think ahead about possible resolutions. Sometimes the only time you can choose the termination option is when you sign the initial lease, not when you renew.

GET OUT AND STAY OUT!

It's probably the last thing you want to think about when you're moving in, but if you know a little about how **eviction** works, you'll be prepared if you ever have to face it. Every state has its own particular laws, but almost all of them require that your landlord give you written notice and prove in court that you've done something that's worthy of eviction.

A landlord can give you three different kinds of eviction notices:

- A **pay or quit notice** means that you'll face eviction if you don't pay your late rent
- A **cure or quit notice** means that you've broken one of the terms of your lease, and if you don't remedy it—by getting rid of that unauthorized pet, for example, or turning down your stereo—you'll be evicted
- An **unconditional quit notice** means you're out and don't have the chance to correct what you did wrong

These notices are usually valid only when you've repeatedly been late with the rent or have otherwise broken your lease, or if you've used your apartment illegally in some way, such as running a business out of it.

MOVIN' OUT

If you decide to move out of your place before your lease is up, chances are you'll be leaving some rent behind. That's right—in most states, if you leave early, you've still got to pay for the apartment until the landlord finds a new tenant. And it's not impossible that you might end up being

continue to evolve, helping to guarantee equal access to housing and eviction protection as well as to plumbing, heating, and other necessities.

85

Renter's Insurance

Even if you're living in a rental, don't live without a net.

One of the great things about renting instead of buying is that you don't have to deal with the commitment of making a long-term investment. But that doesn't mean your home doesn't have value, or that this value isn't vulnerable. After all, even if you don't own the space itself, it holds most of your personal property. Plus, as the tenant, you're liable for what happens there. That's why it's a smart idea to get **renter's insurance**. It's a relatively affordable way to get some peace of mind along with legal and financial security.

IT'S A SLIPPERY SLOPE

Despite what you might think, your landlord's insurance policy doesn't cover everything in your residence. In fact, it covers the place itself, but nothing more. So if a leaky roof floods your living room, you won't have to pay for repairs to the floor, walls, or other parts of the dwelling, but you *will* be stuck with the cost of replacing or repairing anything that you lose as a result of the flood.

And if that flood is your fault—say, from a faucet you left on while you were taking a nap—you're liable for *all* of the damage that's done. And what if a guest slips in that water and breaks a leg? Hopefully he or she has health insurance. However, since you created the hazard, you're liable for the injury, and the health insurance company can legally try to recover its costs from you. In the worst case, your (former) friend could even sue you for negligence.

RUN FOR COVERAGE

If you don't have insurance protection, accidents can leave you broke. Fortunately, renter's insurance offers an easy and affordable way to protect yourself from all sorts of losses, both inside and outside of your home.

Renter's insurance can protect you in two ways:

Loss and damage. Renter's insurance covers your possessions against losses from fire and smoke, theft, vandalism, lightning, wind, explosion, and water damage from plumbing. Your things are also covered away from home—say, if you're on vacation and lose a bag—for anywhere from 10% to their full value, depending on your policy. You're also covered under most standard policies for any items that are in your possession, such as movies you've rented or clothes you've borrowed from friends.

Some insurance companies set limits for coverage on some valuable items, such as computers or jewelry, but most other things are fully covered under most policies. Certain policies even cover cash losses. But remember, making lots of claims can boost the cost of your policy, or even risk having it cancelled.

Liability. Renter's insurance covers your liability for other people injured at your home or by your pets. It also covers you for any legal costs you might incur if you get hit with a liability lawsuit.

TAKE STOCK

If you want to get renter's insurance, the first thing you should do is take an inventory of your home and your possessions so that you know how big a policy you need.

Don't be too conservative. While it may seem at first glance like you own very little of value, it's not uncommon to end up with a total of $15,000 to $20,000 or more. You should also be sure to record whatever inventory you take. Make a note of the model and serial numbers of all your expensive appliances and electronics, get written valuations of jewelry or family heirlooms, and

describe your collection of baseball cards in detail. It can't hurt to take pictures of your possessions, or even record them on videotape. Then store this record someplace safe outside of your apartment—maybe at your office, or in a safe deposit box at your bank.

Once you have a sense of how much coverage you'll need, look around for an insurance company to provide a policy. If you already have car insurance, or you're planning to get it, many companies will offer you a discount if you take out both policies with them.

HOW IT WORKS

Renter's insurance works pretty much the same as other forms of insurance. You pay a **premium**, and if any of the losses covered under your policy occur, you file a claim and the insurance company compensates you for any cost over your **deductible**, up to your policy's limit.

Premiums for renter's insurance are usually inexpensive, anywhere from $75 to $250 a year depending on the company and the type and size of policy. Accepting a higher deductible usually lowers your premium, which can be a smart move if most of the things that matter to you are pretty expensive.

If you have a loss that's covered by your policy, you get paid back in one of two ways, depending on the policy. If you have an **actual cash value** policy, you'll get reimbursed for what the item is worth when it's damaged or lost. So, for example, if you have a stereo that's five years old, you wouldn't get a lot of money back for it. Fortunately, most companies these days offer **replacement value** policies, which pay for what a similar item would cost today—so you'd get enough money back to buy a new stereo.

RENTER'S INSURANCE

WHAT'S NOT COVERED

Renter's insurance doesn't protect you against everything—damage from certain natural disasters such as floods and earthquakes isn't covered under most policies. When you're shopping for insurance, read each policy closely to make sure you know what is and isn't covered. If you think you're at risk for something that's not included in the policy you're thinking about buying, look further or consider getting an additional policy to give you the special protection you need.

Living with Company

Living with roommates means sharing more than just space.

It's common to have a roommate when you're starting out. In addition to the company the person provides, having someone else to share rent and other expenses can make it a lot easier to stay on top of housing costs. But having a roommate comes with potential financial and legal issues. And since there's always the chance that you and your roommate might end up having some personal problems as well, you should know where you stand legally before you sign a joint lease.

Joint

Subletting

ONE FOR ALL AND ALL FOR ONE

In most cases, your lease will state that you and your roommates are all "jointly and severally liable" for the rent, security deposit, and any other costs that come up as a result of renting the property. This means that you're all **lessees**—that's the legal term for the people who sign the lease—and you're all responsible for each others' actions. So if one of you isn't able to pay the rent, causes serious damage to the place, or violates the lease in any other way, the landlord can legally evict all of you, not just the guilty party. That can mean a black mark on your credit history, as well as the cost and difficulty of having to find a new place to live.

Of course, what actually happens in a situation like that is another story. For example, if your roommate loses a job and can't pay, you could always choose to cover his or her share of the rent rather than leaving yourself at the mercy of your landlord. Or, your landlord might cut those of you that aren't at fault a little slack, deciding that it's better to keep you than look for a new tenant. But the offending roommate may still have to go.

SUBLETTING

If your landlord allows it, you—or one of your roommates—can sign the lease and be the official renter, with everybody else **subletting**, or renting a portion of the place, from the single lessee.

Most sublets happen when one person rents part of a residence from somebody who's already living there, but there's no reason why you can't set up a sublet relationship with everyone moving in at the same time.

The advantage of subletting is that it lets you set up an official chain of financial responsibility. Say that you're the **sublessor**, the one with your name on the lease, and your **sublessee**, the roommate who's renting from you, can't pay the rent or does something else that breaks your lease. You're legally entitled to evict him or her, or to use part of his or her security deposit to pay the rent or other resulting expenses until the situation changes. This way, you can't legally be evicted because of something that your sublessee does.

While subletting sounds great in theory, there can be problems. The key is often the relationship you have with the other people involved. For example, you might find it hard to take action

Contracts

Notarized Roommate Contract

against a sublessee who's a friend. And of course, it can be even worse if *you're* the sublessee when a sublessor runs into financial trouble.

CONTRACTS
If your landlord doesn't allow subletting, you can always write a **roommate contract** that spells out everyone's obligations to each other as cotenants. Make sure you specify how much rent each person will pay and when it will be paid. Then get it notarized so that it's a legal document. Many lawyers and real estate brokers, as well as copy centers and stationery stores, provide notary services at low costs. If you have a dispute with a roommate over something that's outlined in your contract, you can take that person to court if you need to.

Make sure any contract with your roommates is written and signed if you're serious about keeping it in force.

Having an actual copy of your agreement will make everyone involved a lot more likely to take it seriously. And if somebody reneges, a written document may hold up in court, while an oral agreement may not.

SKIPPING OUT EARLY
If one of your roommates wants to leave before the lease is up, you're technically required to notify your landlord and either cover the rent yourself or find a new tenant to be responsible under the terms of the lease.

But unless your building is pretty strict, you can probably just line up another tenant without having to notify your landlord at all—most landlords won't worry too much as long as the rent keeps coming in. Of course, until you find another roommate, you'll be responsible for your ex-roommate's share (unless he or she is *very* generous and helpful). And if anything goes wrong with the apartment and your new roommate isn't on the lease, chances are you'll have to take full responsibility.

If you can't afford to keep your place until you find a new roommate, or if you just want to get out of a bad situation, you might want to move out as well. In that case, let your landlord know in writing and be as flexible as you can in helping to find new tenants. The sooner you do, the sooner you'll stop being liable for the rent, and the less likely your landlord will be to take money out of your security deposit or threaten you with eviction for nonpayment.

My new landlord made one emphatic request when my roommate and I moved in—he wanted only one check for the full amount of our rent each month. At first, it was difficult for my roommate and me to trust each other—neither of us could afford to pay the full rent and not get reimbursed for half. So far, we've been alternating month by month who writes the full check to the landlord and who reimburses the check-writer, and we haven't run into problems.
—Starr M., 23

Why Buy?

A home you buy has a double identity: It's a place to live and an investment.

Even if buying a home is one of your financial goals, you might not be thinking about it for the immediate future.

But more young people are buying homes than you might expect—in fact, almost 1.5 million people under 25 are homeowners, as are almost 40% of people from ages 25 to 29. And they're buying for a smart reason: When you add up the tax breaks and the potential increase in value that it can provide, owning a home can offer substantial financial advantages in addition to all the intangible benefits it offers. That's why buying when you're young can be a smart way to get a head start on your financial life.

TAX TIPS

If you're making a lot of money, your parents, your accountant, and anybody else with financial experience is probably telling you that buying a house will be a great tax break. That's because the interest you pay on a mortgage is usually tax deductible, as is all the money you pay in real estate taxes.

If you really want to see the savings that this tax break provides, think about it in comparison to renting. If you're spending as much on your mortgage as

LOST IN SPACE
Another advantage of buying over renting is that you usually get a lot more space for your money. That's definitely a bonus, especially if you're living with a partner, spouse, or friend.

you would on rent—which is a fairly reasonable expectation in a lot of cases—a percentage of the portion that goes to interest ends up back in your pocket, while with rent it all stays with the landlord. And since you pay a larger proportion of interest early on with most mortgages, you'll be getting an even larger break in the first few years.

For example, if you had a 30-year $100,000 mortgage with an APR of 6.5%, you'd pay almost $6,500 in interest during the first year you owned your home. You could include that amount in your itemized deductions, along with some of the costs of buying. Itemized deductions are subtracted from your adjusted gross income to reduce your taxable income. Itemizing your real estate taxes would reduce your taxable income—and your taxes—even further.

SELF-HELP
Another advantage to owning your home is that every improvement you make increases its value for you, not your landlord. Even if you're not making huge renovations or additions, every time you get something major replaced or add something permanent to the house, you'll reap the benefits in several ways if you ever want to sell or borrow against your home:

- The money you put in increases the value, so you can often sell at a higher price

HOME EQUITY

- The more the house is worth, the more your equity in it is worth
- When you calculate your profit on the sale of the house, you can use the cost of permanent improvements to increase your **cost basis**, which in turn reduces your capital gain and the threat of owing capital gains tax

That's a lot better than leaving behind the fruits of your labor—and your money—when you move to another rental.

Owning a home can give you a tax break on the selling end as well. If you sell a property that's your primary home for more than what you paid for it plus the cost of any improvements you made, you have a **capital gain**. As long as you've lived there for at least two of the five years before you sell, and you haven't sold or exchanged another home in the past two years, you're allowed to exclude up to $250,000 of that gain if you're single, and up to $500,000 if you're married. That translates into $37,500 or $75,000 in tax savings, figured at the long-term capital gains rate of 15%.

YOUR HOME AS AN INVESTMENT

As you pay off your mortgage, you build up more and more **equity**, or ownership, in your home, and it becomes more and more valuable to you as an investment. And while a mortgage can seem like forever when the term is longer than you've been alive, when it ends the house is all yours.

If it increases in value at any point, including while you're still paying that mortgage, you can sell it for a profit. And, while most other investments don't give you anything tangible while you own them, real estate gives you a place to live or work.

But though real estate prices often rise, they don't always—so there's risk involved, just as with any other investment. And if you're trying to sell in a slow market, you'll have a harder time finding a buyer for a house than for a stock or bond.

MOVIN' ON UP

One more good thing about buying a home is that it makes it easier to buy another one in the future—often a nicer,

more expensive one. For one thing, as long as you keep on top of your mortgage payments, you'll develop a strong credit history. That'll go a long way toward getting you the larger mortgage you'll need for a bigger house, especially if you didn't have much of a history before your first house.

Selling your first home for a profit can also help you trade up to a more expensive one. This is where any improvements you make will hopefully increase the value of your home above what you paid for it. But don't stake too much on a big price increase, especially in the short term. And investigate the types of improvements that typically pay off in higher prices.

The Home Runaround

You've got to cover a lot of bases to buy a home safely.

Lining up all the necessary pieces to buy a home can take a lot of legwork. You've got to figure out what you can spend, what you want to buy, and how you're going to pay for it—and not necessarily in that order. It's a much more involved process than renting. But it comes with a much bigger payoff, personally as well as financially.

BALLPARK FIGURES

If you're like most people, the key to buying is getting a **mortgage**, a long-term loan that you can repay over an extended period, typically 15 or 30 years. While there are no hard and fast rules, most lenders use criteria set by **Fannie Mae** and **Freddie Mac**, corporations that buy mortgages from lenders, to evaluate whether you're a good candidate for a mortgage.

The first test asks if you've got enough regular income to afford the payments. Lenders say you shouldn't be spending more than 28% of your pretax income on housing. So if you make $3,500 a month, you can spend $980 of that on your mortgage, taxes, and insurance. Sometimes if you make a big down payment, you can get away with paying a larger portion of your income every month. Or you may qualify for a government sponsored program that relaxes the normal guidelines.

Even if your income puts you within that 28% range for the mortgage you're looking for, you've still got to prove you don't have too much debt hiding in the background. No more than 36% of your monthly income can go to all of your debts together. That means you can be using $1,260 of a $3,500 salary to cover your mortgage plus your credit card balance, student loans, and any other debt. You can see how interest on cards could be a big problem here—so make sure your spending is under control before you go looking for a house.

A steady job and a good credit history are also crucial to getting through the mortgage process successfully. All in all, if you're a good candidate, you should be able to afford a house that costs about 2½ times your annual salary. If you and a partner or spouse are buying jointly, both of your incomes count toward this standard.

START YOUR SEARCH

If a rough idea of what you can afford is enough for you to go on—and for many people it is—you can jump right into the search by contacting a real estate **broker**.

Since they have good knowledge of different areas and the properties that are available in them, brokers can make your search a lot easier. But as you'll probably know if you've dealt with brokers while looking for a rental, they're trying to get the highest prices possible for the sellers they represent, which means you could end up paying top dollar.

Brokers usually show you only what you can afford, since they'll lose a sale if you don't qualify for what you're looking at. But they won't negotiate actively on your behalf to get a lower price. For that, you need a **buyer's agent**, whose job is to get you a good deal on the purchase price or better contract terms.

SHOW ME THE MONEY

It can be a little nerve-wracking to go house hunting without knowing the size of the mortgage you'll ultimately qualify for. One way to get around that uncertainty is to try to be preapproved for a mortgage. That means you apply for a mortgage before you start looking for a house, so that you'll know whether you'll be able to borrow, and how much.

There's not always an opportunity to for preapproval—lenders usually offer preapproved mortgages only when they've got a surplus of cash to lend. But when they do, it can be a great way to make your shopping process a little easier.

PAYMENT

ADJUSTED MORTGAGE FIXED

Knowing where you stand can help you out in a number of ways. First and foremost, you'll be able to streamline your search to include only properties within your price range. And you can bid on those properties with the confidence that you can afford them.

Also, having a loan already lined up cuts down on delays in the buying process, so you can sometimes get a sweeter deal since you'll be saving the seller some time and trouble. Applying for a prequalified mortgage does cost money, though, so make sure you're serious about buying before you start.

MORTGAGE CHOICES

As you're looking for mortgages, make sure you know which kind will work best for you. If you want to be able to budget for your current and future payments, go for a **fixed-rate mortgage**. That way you'll always know what you owe, no matter what's going on with your finances or the economy at large. For example, if you lose your job, or go back to school, or if anything else happens that would change your cash flow, at least you can be sure that your payments won't go any higher.

If it's more important to you to have low payments early on—if you have a lower-paying job than you expect to

have later, for example, or if you have a huge student loan burden—think about an **adjustable-rate mortgage (ARM)**. The rates on these mortgages usually start out lower than on fixed-rate loans, which may mean you can afford a somewhat more expensive house.

You could end up paying more with an ARM than with a fixed-rate loan, though, if interest rates go higher in the future. But you never know—you could always end up paying less.

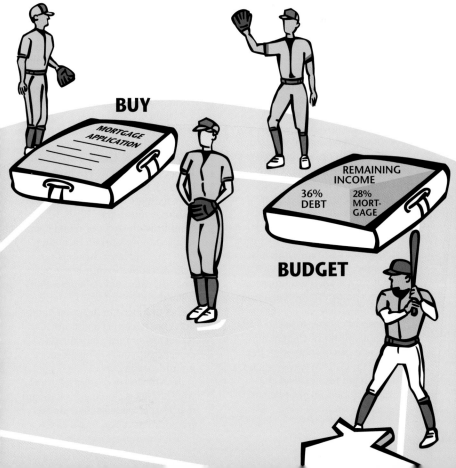

BUY

MORTGAGE APPLICATION

REMAINING INCOME

36% DEBT   28% MORTGAGE

BUDGET

Home Insurance

If you're buying a home, you'll want to protect your investment.

Buying a home is never financially easy, especially when you're young. But one of the things that makes it worthwhile is the fact that—unlike with a rental— the money you spend on it becomes an investment.

That's why home insurance is so important. Without it, if your home is damaged or destroyed, you lose the place you live in as well as whatever it's worth. But if you have insurance, you'll be able to rebuild both your home and the financial security it provides.

Even if you don't think insurance is a good idea, you're stuck with it anyway. Lenders require you to have it. That way they're protected from any loss, especially in the early years of a mortgage when most of the equity—and the risk—is theirs.

HOW IT WORKS

Home insurance works the same way renter's insurance and other forms of insurance do. You pay a regular **premium** for the privilege of being covered. If your

home is damaged, you're responsible for covering any repairs up to the amount of your **deductible**. After that, your insurance kicks in and reimburses you for as much of the damage as your policy allows. The larger the deductible, the less you'll have to pay for each premium—but of course you'll have to pay more out of your own pocket if your house is ever damaged.

WHAT COVERS WHAT

Home insurance comes in different levels of coverage, labeled from H01 to H08, with higher numbers signifying broader and more comprehensive coverage. For example, H01 covers only a set list of **perils**, such as fire, wind, and hail. Higher levels protect you from other threats, like damage and theft, and can cover you against liability for injuries and accidents that happen on your property.

But basic policies don't usually cover against larger disasters, like earthquakes or floods. For that, you'll either need to purchase separate policies or pay for special **riders**, which function as amendments to your main policy. Different riders can vary drastically in cost depending on where you live. For example, earthquake insurance is cheap in the midwest, but expensive in California. And the opposite is true for tornado and flood insurance.

HOW MUCH DO YOU NEED?

If you want to figure out how much coverage you should have, first you have to figure out the **replacement value** of your home. That's what it would cost to repair or rebuild your home at today's prices, including materials and labor. Insurers can help you appraise your home to find this value, but remember that it's in their best interest to arrive at a high number. On the other hand, don't be shocked at a number that seems higher than you expect, especially if you're living in an up-and-coming area.

It's wise to cover at least 80% of your home's replacement value, and many experts advise covering the whole amount. You might also want

TAKE NOTES!

If your home is ever damaged, you'll have a much easier time recovering money from your insurance provider if you've kept good records of your valuable possessions. Write down the purchase price and date, manufacturer, model, vendor, and the serial number of all your expensive items. Keeping receipts is a good idea too.

In fact, if you can record your possessions with photographs or video, you'll be even safer. That way, if anything is damaged, you can shoot it again for comparison.

And of course, make sure to keep all of this documentation in a safe place—one other than your house. That way you'll be able to get to it easily if anything happens to your house.

MY HOUSE

to add the value of the belongings in your home into your replacement value if you want them covered as well—especially if you own a lot of expensive things like electronics, jewelry, antiques, or collectibles.

CHECK THE DETAILS

Many insurance companies offer to cover the **market value** of your home, which is the price you'd get if you sold it in the current market. Since market value includes the value of the land around your house—which rarely needs to be insured—you'll be paying to insure a higher amount than you really need to.

And if you're insuring your belongings, make sure they're insured for **replacement value**, not **cash value**. The cash value of belongings is what you could get from selling them at the present time. And since expensive things like appliances depreciate over time, cash value is usually a lot less than replacement value. That means you'll have to lay out money of your own if you want to replace destroyed or damaged items.

So while it can sometimes be a little more expensive to cover your house and belongings for replacement value, the protection it provides against the forces of inflation and the fluctuation of real estate prices is usually well worth it in the long run.

INSURING CONDOS AND CO-OPS

If you own an apartment in a condominium or a co-op, you're living inside a structure and on property that's not entirely owned by you. But you can—and should—still insure your home.

You can get protection for your possessions and liability, much as you would with renter's insurance. And you can get additional coverage for the walls, floors, and ceilings of your property. The condominium owner or co-op board should cover the outer walls of the building.

In the House

It helps to know the ins and outs of home finance.

WHAT'S IN A RENT PAYMENT?

When you're budgeting for rent, make sure you know what a monthly payment covers. Landlords in different areas include specific things in the price of rent. For example, in some cities, landlords are required to provide heat, hot water, and utilities. Elsewhere, you're required to pay for some or all of these services on top of the rent—as

well as arrange for them. Hidden costs like these can tack on as much as a few hundred dollars a month to what you pay for housing, so make sure you're aware of them as you start to plan.

CAR AND RENTER'S INSURANCE

If you've got a car, it's not covered under renter's insurance, even though it's one of your possessions. Since there's more risk and higher value involved, cars require their own separate insurance policies. In fact, car insurance isn't just a good idea—it's required by law.

POLICIES FOR TWO (OR MORE)

Most states allow you to take out a joint renter's insurance policy with one or more roommates or with an unmarried partner. Not all companies offer joint coverage, though, so shop around for something that meets your needs. When you're ready to sign, make sure that each person's name is included on the policy so that you're all guaranteed coverage.

INSTEAD OF GETTING THE CHINA

If you're getting married and you're considering buying a house soon, think about setting up a bridal registry with the **Federal Housing Administration (FHA)**. Your friends and family can contribute toward a down payment on a home you buy using an FHA mortgage.

Some of your guests might not feel comfortable giving money for a purchase rather than a gift, as they would in traditional registries. But if you feel like a step toward a home would be more important to you than a toaster oven or another pair of candlesticks, you might want to think about including this option, even if you pair it with a traditional registry.

OFFICE

GARAGE

LIVING ROOM

RENTER'S INSURANCE
Joint Coverage

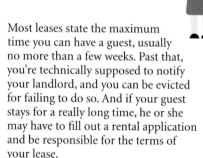

UTILITY COST-CUTTING

It's easy to forget to include utilities when you're thinking about home finance costs. But when you factor in electricity, gas, heat, phones, and other costs, the total can be surprisingly high. A little care and research can be helpful in keeping these costs down:

- Keep air conditioning and heat off when you're not home, or set them on a timer to regulate how much they're used
- Shop around for the best phone calling plan, and make the effort to switch plans if it's going to save you money
- If you have a cell phone with lots of free minutes, consider using it as your main phone to avoid fees on a land line
- If you have a dishwasher, use it to wash your dishes—it uses over a third less hot water than doing them by hand—but not to dry them, since it uses a lot of electricity

GUEST OR TENANT?

Having guests in your apartment is a gray area in terms of leases and legality.

Most leases state the maximum time you can have a guest, usually no more than a few weeks. Past that, you're technically supposed to notify your landlord, and you can be evicted for failing to do so. And if your guest stays for a really long time, he or she may have to fill out a rental application and be responsible for the terms of your lease.

Of course, whether any of this will happen is another story. If your landlord is fairly lax, there's no reason why you can't have a guest—a person you're in a relationship with, say, or a friend from school who's looking for an apartment and a job—for as long as you want. Just remember that having a long-term guest in your house will probably cost you money in terms of utilities, wear and tear on the apartment, and groceries. And then there's always what it costs in terms of your patience.

RULES FOR ROOMMATES

If you're living with one or more roommates, it's common to have some difficulties about how to handle sharing costs. There's no sure-fire way to avoid this, but there are systems you can set up for taking care of household expenses:

- Keep a jar where everyone puts receipts and bills for what they spend on household items and settle up differences every week or every month
- Have a different person take responsibility for the bills and/or shopping each month
- Break your regular household expenses down into relatively equal groups, and have each person pay for one group

These aren't the only methods out there, and there may be another that works better for you and your roommates, depending on your financial situations and how careful you want to be about keeping things even. All that really matters is that you find a system that works for everyone and stick to it.

Play Your Cards Right

Whether you want to cash out in a few years or a few decades, you've got to ante up now.

While you often hear people your parents' age talking about planning their financial future, it probably doesn't come up as much when you're around your friends. But just because it's not the main topic of conversation doesn't mean you shouldn't be setting up a **financial plan**.

Simply put, a financial plan is a written statement of your financial goals and your strategy for achieving them. It includes a list of your current assets and how they're invested. And it lays out a schedule for making additional investments.

FUTURE SHOCK
Getting yourself energized to do financial planning takes determination. If you have a good job, you can usually manage fine from paycheck to paycheck, and you might even be able to cover a larger expense, such as a mortgage, without too much trouble.

But at some point—whether you're having kids, going back to school, or retiring—the things you want or need to pay for will outdistance what you have in your pocket or your bank account. And if you haven't planned for those costs, you may find yourself having to postpone or abandon things you've been looking forward to for a long time.

In fact, the sooner you get started, the better. That's because you'll have more years to put money away. Plus, the more time you have, the more **compounding** can help your money grow. Compounding occurs when your earnings are reinvested to form a new, larger base on which future earnings accumulate.

THE LONG AND SHORT (AND MEDIUM) OF IT

You've probably got a range of goals in mind for the future. They can be as immediate and as simple as a vacation next summer or as far off and large-scale as a comfortable retirement. The trick is to figure out how to balance all those potentially conflicting needs and their various time frames.

If you plan your investing—and make your investment choices—to give you what you need when you need it, you're a lot less likely to find yourself scrambling to reach your goals, or missing out altogether.

For example, if you're focused on events in the near future, like buying a new car or getting married, you'll want to put your money into investments that are easily accessible and aren't so vulnerable to loss of value. But for goals further down the road, you can afford to take a little more risk when you invest, since you have more time to recover from any setbacks. In fact, since those distant goals are usually the more expensive ones—like providing for a child's education or buying a second home—planning and investing isn't just a good idea, it's usually a necessity.

Think about starting small—maybe set up an automatic deduction from your paycheck, even if it's only $25 or $50. That way, you don't have to worry about going to the bank or jumping online here and there to do stuff. I tried to keep a schedule at first...told myself that I'd invest a certain amount every quarter. Yeah, right! When you're busy, it's tough to keep up with even the most well-intended schedule.

—George C., 26

Of course, there's no reason you can't change your goals and your plans for achieving them as your life changes. For example, if you decide to go back to school, you may put your plans for a house or family on the back burner. Or if you decide to have kids or start your own business, you may decide to reevaluate your insurance needs or alter your investment style. Whatever you're doing or wherever you are in life, it's a good idea to assess your financial plan about once a year.

ACES IN THE HOLE

So what's the trick to creating a financial plan that will help you get where you want? Picking the actual investments that will take you there is a different process for each person, but there are some general rules that apply across the board. If you plan well, you should be able to:

Outpace inflation. You need to put your money into investments with rates of return that will make money faster than the current inflation rate, which has averaged 3% since 1926. That way you'll be able to afford the things you're planning for when the time comes.

Keep taxes low. Taxes can eat away at the earnings your investments provide. But putting your money in a tax-deferred investment like a 401(k) or an IRA, or a tax-exempt investment like a Roth IRA, can protect some of your money from that bite.

Be ready for a rainy day. Creating an easily accessible emergency fund can help keep your financial plans from getting wiped out by unexpected problems like illness or unemployment.

Spotting the Right Car

If you survey the car scene, you can identify a model that meets your needs if not your dreams.

Consumers buy or lease more than 1.66 million new cars in the US each year. That's roughly one for every 17 people. While it may be comforting to know that other people are coping with the same issues of sticker price and payment options, there's no way around the fact that buying a car means making a big financial commitment.

WHAT CAN YOU AFFORD?

Unless money is no object, you'll want to know how much you can spend before you start shopping seriously for a car. You'll need:

- Enough cash for a down payment, often 10% to 20% of the purchase price
- A regular source of income so you can keep up with monthly payments
- Money to cover insurance and regular upkeep

TAKE THE OFFENSIVE

One way to start the search process is to investigate **preapproval** for a loan. You complete and submit a short application, either online, at your bank, or at a car dealer, to find out exactly how much money a lender is willing to let you borrow—although you don't have any obligation to take the loan. You might even want to shop around for the best offer on preapproved loans. Be aware of the potential charges for preapproval, though. It's often free, but some lenders charge a small fee, which can add up if you apply to multiple loan sources.

TRANSPORTATION OPTIONS

Depending on where you live, having a car might be a necessity. But if you don't absolutely need one, there can be other ways to get around. Living in an urban or suburban area with a good mass transit or commuter rail system can save you a lot of money every month. And some employers offer the chance to take public transportation expenses out of your paycheck tax free, making it a great alternative to owning a car.

THE SECOND TIME AROUND

Although used cars can be a bit less glamorous than brand new models, you can almost always get more car for your money. That's because **depreciation**—the decrease of a car's value over time—can claim 10% to 40% of a new car's value in the first year alone. So you can often get a great deal on a car if you don't mind that someone else has driven it for a while.

In fact, a luxury car that's just a few years old can cost about the same as a new economy car. But remember, expensive cars can often cost more to maintain and insure, even if they're several years old.

Even if you think a used car is in perfect shape, you should do some

WHAT SHOULD YOU PAY?

Your biggest challenge probably won't be finding the car you want to buy, but paying the price you want to pay.

As weird as it may sound, a new car actually has several different prices. The highest one is usually the **manufacturer's suggested retail price (MSRP)**, which is the number you see on the sticker in the car's window. That's the price the seller would like you to pay.

The car also has an **invoice price**. That's the official amount the manufacturer charges the dealer for the car. It includes the cost of building, transporting, storing, displaying, maintaining, and advertising the car.

There's also the **actual price**, which is the amount the dealer really paid. In most cases, it's lower than the invoice price because of rebates or other incentives the manufacturer offers the dealer, promotions the manufacturer pays for, or **holdbacks**, the part of the cost that covers running the dealership.

And then there's the **sale price**—the amount you pay. Most dealers are willing to negotiate a price between their actual cost and the MSRP,

READ UP

Before trying to negotiate the price of a car, you can get current invoice information, which includes details on rebates, factory-to-dealer incentives, and holdbacks, from Consumer Reports (800-933-5555) or from the new vehicles section of www.edmunds.com.

Consumer Reports and several automotive magazines also publish annual guides to buying new and used cars with ratings, comparisons, and reviews of just about every car on the market. And you can find all of this information over the Web, sometimes for a fee and sometimes for free. For starters, check out www.cars.com, www.cartalk.cars.com, www.carsmart.com, and www.autobytel.com.

except when the model you're buying is very popular and in high demand.

You've got to be the one who initiates the bargaining, though. And you have to make it clear you've done your research and know what the real numbers are.

checking. Ask the person or dealership selling the car for **repair records** and any **title history** they have before you get your heart set—or put your money down—on the car.

If the seller doesn't have any records, you can get a car's complete title history for free over the Internet at www.carfax.com. You'll need the **vehicle identification number (VIN)**, which appears in the lower left corner of the windshield, and your zip code.

20%

APPROVED

PAY
STUB

LOAN
APPLICATION

Loan or Lease?

Once you've found the car you want, you've got to think about how to pay for it.

Buying—whether you're spending your own money or taking a loan, also known as **financing**—is the traditional way to get a car, but it isn't the only way. You can also **lease** a car for a monthly fee. When the lease ends, usually after three or four years, you return the car to the **lessor**, or the company leasing you the vehicle.

Leasing has several appealing factors: You usually don't have to put a lot of money down, your monthly payments are smaller than they would be with a loan, and you can change cars every few years.

On the other hand, you never own a car that you lease, so you can't sell it or trade it in for a new one if you want. When the lease ends, you have to arrange another lease or buy a car. And, your insurance costs may be higher than they would be on a comparable car that you owned outright.

THE TERMS OF A LEASE

When you buy a car, you agree on a price with the dealer. Similarly, when you lease, you negotiate a price, called the **capitalization cost**. In most cases, that amount should be less—hopefully significantly less—than the manufacturer's suggested retail price (MSRP).

Your **monthly payment** is what the lease costs each month, including sales tax. These payments remain the same for the term of the lease.

Once you've paid all of your monthly payments, what's left is the car's **residual value**. It's figured as a percentage of the MSRP, based on how comparable cars depreciate in the time covered by the lease. If you want to buy

WHEN YOU BUY WITH A LOAN

PROS

- You own your car when the loan is paid
- You can get full financing if you qualify
- You can take advantage of special promotions
- You have no mileage limits

CONS

- You may have to make a large down payment
- You owe sales tax on the purchase price up front
- You absorb the depreciation of the car
- After the warranty runs out, you are responsible for everything that could go wrong with the car

the car when the lease ends, you'll have to pay this amount regardless of what the car is actually worth at that point.

That cost is the main reason you should think twice about leasing if there's any real possibility you'll end up buying the car when the lease ends. It would almost always be cheaper to finance the purchase from the start.

There's also an **acquisition fee** on top of your initial payment. The amount varies, based on the car you're leasing and the lessor. It covers credit reports and other paperwork.

When you sign a lease, you agree to **mileage limits**—usually around 12,000 to 15,000 a year. You'll have to pay 10 to 15 cents for every mile you drive over that limit.

Some leases also include a **regular termination fee**, which covers charges for wear and tear on the car and any excess mileage. And, finally, many dealers charge a **disposition fee** to pay for the costs of reselling the car after the lease is finished.

LEASING SMARTS

When you lease a car, you have to qualify for credit, just as you would if you were taking a loan. And you have to sign a lease agreement that spells out the terms and conditions. The more you know about how leases work, the better the deal you can arrange. For more information, check out www.leasesource.com.

www.leasesource.com

WHEN YOU LEASE

- You can get a new car every few years
- Your monthly payments are usually lower than loan payments
- You can get a more expensive car for less than it would cost to buy one
- Depreciation isn't your problem unless you end up buying the car

- Residual value may be set artificially high to lower payments during the term of the lease, making purchase expensive
- You have set mileage limits
- You may be penalized for not keeping the car in perfect condition
- Your agreement with the lessor is hard to break

THE COST OF A LEASE

You have to pay your first and last monthly payments and a security deposit up front on a lease. You may also have to make a down payment, or deposit. Also known as the **capitalized cost reduction**, that deposit lowers your monthly payments—but not the overall cost of the lease.

PAYING TOO SOON

If you want to get out of a car loan early—for example, if you want to pay off the entire amount before the end of the term—you may get hit with a **prepayment penalty**, which is a lump-sum charge on top of the outstanding principal. That's because if you pay off what you owe before the term is up, you save money on interest but the lender loses that income.

It's usually more difficult, and more expensive, to try to end a lease agreement early. In most cases, the penalty you have to pay will be substantial, sometimes the full amount remaining on the lease. The only way to avoid it is to roll over the lease on your current car to a lease on a newer or more expensive car from the same lessor.

What a Car Loan Costs

Gearing up to get a car loan is the key to getting wheels.

When you're shopping for a car loan, remember that what it costs you to borrow depends on three things:

- The finance charge, expressed as an **annual percentage rate (APR)**
- The **term**, or length of time the loan lasts
- The **principal**, or amount you borrow

THE APR

The **APR** is a percentage of the loan principal that you must pay to your credit union, bank, or other lender every year to finance the purchase of your car. This **finance charge** includes interest and any fees for arranging the loan. The charge gets added to the amount you borrow, and you repay the combined total, typically in monthly installments over the course of the term.

For example, if you take a $15,000 auto loan from your credit union with a 7.5% APR that you repay over four years, you'll owe $362.69 every month. Over a year, those payments would total $4,352.28, and over the life of the loan, $17,409.12. That means it costs you $2,409.12 to borrow the money to buy the car.

When you're looking for a loan, you want the lowest APR you can find for the term you choose. The higher the rate, the more borrowing will cost you.

Most APRs you'll be offered will be in the same ballpark. That's because the cost of borrowing at any given time depends on what lenders themselves have to pay for the money they're using to make loans. But credit unions, which aren't trying to make a profit, or the financing arms of car companies that want to promote the sale of their cars, might offer lower rates.

You may even find that rates from car companies are as low as 0%—especially if sales have been sluggish and they're trying to entice buyers. Obviously it can be a good deal. But be careful to read the fine print about the conditions that may apply.

THE TERM

The term of your loan also affects what it costs you to borrow. A shorter term means higher monthly payments but a

$15,000 LOAN

TERM

APR

Term: 4 years APR: 7.5 % =$362.69/month **$17,409.12 total**	Term: 4 years APR: 9 % =$373.28/month **$17,917.44 total**
Term: 3 years APR: 7.5 % =$466.60/month **$16,797.60 total**	
Term: 5 years APR: 7.5 % =$300.57/month **$18,034.20 total**	

NOT-SO-HIDDEN COSTS

When you're shopping for a car, you have to take costs beyond the sale price into consideration. You'll be responsible for sales tax on the full amount of the purchase, fees for the title and registration, and insurance payments. And you're legally obligated to have car insurance in all 50 states. In fact, you can't get a loan without it.

BALLOON LOANS

You might hear about **balloon loans** as you shop around for car financing. These loans require you to pay just interest, generally calculated at an average rate for the term of the loan, and then make a large final payment of the outstanding principal.

This style of payment can seem attractive, especially if you don't have the money for a down payment on a regular loan. But it's also extremely risky. If you can't pay the final amount, you might have to take out another loan to pay the final installment—or worse, your car could be repossessed.

lower total cost. On the flip side, a longer term means smaller monthly payments and a higher total cost.

For example, the same $15,000 loan at 7.5% APR that cost $362.69 a month for a four-year term would cost $466.60 a month for a three-year term and $300.57 for a five-year term. But the three-year term would cost you just $1,797.60 in finance charges—$611.52 less than the four-year loan. And the loan with the five-year term would cost $3,034.20, or $625.08 more than the one with the four-year term.

Sometimes, though, you still might choose the longer term, and the higher cost, if you can manage the smaller payment more easily than the larger one. After all, it can be worth it to pay a little more over time if you're worried that you might default on your payments.

But keep in mind that a car might start to cost you money for upkeep after it reaches a certain age or you've driven it long distances. You don't want to choose so long a term for your car loan that you'll still be paying it off while also having to pay for major repairs.

THE PRINCIPAL

It should come as no surprise that the more you borrow, the more borrowing will cost. After all, the finance charge is determined by multiplying the interest rate times the principal. So the more you can reduce your principal, the more affordable borrowing will be.

One thing you can do to cut down your overall cost is to make the largest down payment you can afford so that you reduce your interest costs. Looking for a car that will have a good trade-in value, and trading it in while it's still in good condition, will help you save money later on as well.

Keep in mind that the cost of insurance will vary depending on the kind of car you want to buy, your age, gender, and driving record, where you live, the insurance company you choose, and the coverage you want. To home in on the best rates, start by visiting a number of car-related or insurance websites to get a sense of what you'll have to spend.

Getting Married

When you tie the knot, finances and ownership can get tangled.

Marriage is a big step in terms of emotional commitment, and it often means a big financial change as well.

Merging your financial lives can be easier than splitting up the closet space or deciding who takes out the garbage. Or it can be a source of constant tension. The bottom line is that being financially compatible—or finding a way to work out your differences—is essential to a happy marriage.

MERGE AHEAD?

Many married couples own most, if not all, of their investments and possessions jointly. Among other reasons it's so popular is that sharing ownership of the things you acquire can make your marriage more equal. And if you both have a stake in your assets, you may both be more inclined to handle them wisely.

Merging your property and finances isn't always the smartest thing to do, though. If either of you works in a profession that might make you vulnerable to lawsuits or has had trouble with creditors, it may be a better idea to keep your assets separate. That way, if one of you finds yourself in financial trouble, you'll be able to keep the other person's finances secure. Similarly, many financial advisers suggest you each keep the assets you had before getting married in your own names.

HI$**   **HER$

MANAGING MONEY

You'll have to work out a way to handle your household finances. You can adopt one of the conventional methods or experiment until you find a system that works for both of you—recognizing that it might mean surviving some fairly intense discussions. You can try:

- Pooling your earnings in a joint account and paying all bills from that account, including your individual expenses
- Keeping separate accounts but splitting the common expenses, with one of you paying rent or mortgage, for example, and the other making car payments and buying food
- Contributing a percentage of your income to a household account to cover the bills and putting the rest in your own accounts

What happens if one of you makes a lot more money than the other, or if one of you isn't working? It can be a problem, but it's one you should try to discuss frankly, especially if the alternative is nursing feelings of inadequacy or resentment. It might help to acknowledge that your roles could switch if the current breadwinner got sick or lost a job.

or as part of a larger group—for example, you and your siblings. You can sell your share of the asset, but you've usually got to get consent from the other owner(s). And you must split the proceeds of the sale evenly with them. If the other owner is your spouse, the asset is considered marital property and it gets split up if you get divorced. When you or any other owner dies, that share becomes the property of the remaining owner(s).

Tenants by the entirety. You have to be married in order to be tenants by the entirety, which means that you own the property together. As long as you stay married, the property remains both of yours—neither of you can sell without the other's permission. If one of you dies, the other becomes the sole owner of the property. If you get divorced, you become tenants in common. Either of you can sell your half without the other's permission.

Tenants in common. If you and your spouse are tenants in common, you each own a share of the property, usually in equal proportions. Ownership isn't limited to the two of you—any number of people can own property in common. Each of you can sell your share independently and keep all of the profits. If you get divorced, property you and your spouse have in common could be subject to division.

WHO OWNS WHAT (AND HOW)

There are four ways to own property. Each comes with its own rules, which govern ownership for just about every kind of property, from bank accounts to investments and real estate.

Sole ownership. As the name suggests, with sole ownership you alone own the asset, and you're free to sell it or give it away as you wish, including by way of a will or trust. But if you buy something on your own when you're married and then you get divorced, it could be counted as marital property and be subject to division.

Joint tenants with rights of survivorship. Under this form of ownership, you own property equally with two or more people. That could mean owning property with just your spouse

COMMUNITY PROPERTY STATES

You might want to be extra wary of switching your premarital assets to joint ownership if you live in a community property state. In these nine states—Arizona, California, Idaho, Louisiana, Nevada, New Mexico, Texas, Washington, and Wisconsin—you give up the right to own something exclusively in the future once you designate it a joint possession. And anything you earn during your marriage is automatically part of this joint pool. But you can protect what was yours beforehand if you keep it in your own name.

Life Insurance

Even if you don't need to buy life insurance yet, you still need to know about it.

Life insurance isn't something people like to talk about, especially young people. After all, thinking about dying and what happens to family or loved ones after you're gone isn't the easiest thing to do. But if anyone depends on you for financial security, life insurance is something you can't afford to ignore. And even if you're not at that stage in life yet, it's still smart to know what's at stake so you can make the right decision when the time does come.

As you take on   more responsibilities

INSURANCE BASICS

When you purchase a life insurance policy, you're agreeing to pay a regular **premium**, or fee, often on a monthly or quarterly basis. In return, the insurance company agrees to pay a **death benefit** of a certain value to your **beneficiaries** if you die. Most people designate their spouses, partners, or children as beneficiaries, but you can choose anyone you want, such as a parent or a business partner.

So how large a policy do you need? There's no set amount. One rule of thumb says that you should have insurance that's five to seven times your annual salary, while another says ten times your salary is appropriate. One thing is for sure, though: If you're like most young people, you have financial obligations like mortgages and children's tuition ahead of you. So you'll need more insurance than older people who've already paid off those kinds of expenses.

DO YOU NEED IT?

The first question to ask yourself about life insurance is whether you need it. If you're married or if you have children, then you definitely do. It's the only sure way to provide income for your family's financial needs, from funeral expenses to mortgages and education costs.

If you don't have a spouse or kids, or if you're planning to stay single, and there's no one else that depends on you for financial support, then you probably don't need insurance. If you die and leave debts behind, your creditors can try to collect from your estate. But they can't collect from your parents or other people unless those people cosigned the loan agreement.

FOR A TIME OR FOR LIFE

There are two main types of life insurance: **term insurance** and **whole life insurance**. As the name suggests, a term policy covers you for a set period of time, usually 5, 10, 15, or 20 years. Then you must renew it.

NO EXCUSES

Even if you know you should be covered by insurance, it can be even more tempting to put off getting coverage than it is to put off investing. And it's easy to find reasons why there's no rush. Here are some common excuses and why they don't stand up.

You're covered through your job. Most employer-based policies are relatively small if they're offered at all, and they end when you leave the company.

You have an accidental death insurance policy. While you have a greater chance of dying in an accident before you're 35 than after, there are still other ways to die. And accidental death policies often come with strings attached. A regular term or whole life policy will give you much more effective coverage.

You bought coverage through a credit card company or your bank. Offers for life insurance that come with your monthly credit card or bank statement can seem appealing—especially since they're convenient and cheap. But they're not always good coverage. Make sure you know what you're buying before you spend money on an offer like this.

your need for life insurance grows

Since term insurance is much cheaper than whole life, many financial experts recommend it for young people. The limited time frame can be good, too, since it gives you the chance to switch over to a whole life policy in the future, if you choose to.

Other advisers suggest you might want to purchase a whole life policy right away. In addition to providing coverage for life, these policies set aside a portion of each premium payment to accumulate as tax-free savings. You can even use these tax-free dollars to pay your premiums. To help sort out your questions, it may be smart to talk to a fee-only insurance consultant who can explain the pros and cons of each type of insurance.

WHOLE LIFE INSURANCE vs. INVESTMENTS

Even though whole life insurance provides tax-free savings, just as some types of investments do, that doesn't mean that the two things serve the same purpose. Many people make the mistake of thinking that they can provide financial security for their loved ones just by investing. Or they think that they can use the value that builds up in their insurance policy to support themselves in retirement instead of using investments and other savings.

A financial plan that omits insurance or investments can be a dangerous proposition. You run the risk of leaving your loved ones with financial burdens if you die, or of not having the money to retire the way you want, or both. To have a secure financial strategy, you should consider both insurance and investments.

Inheritances

Receiving an inheritance can open a Pandora's box if you don't know how to handle your new assets.

Inheriting a large amount of money or valuable property can change your life, especially if you're young. After all, a sudden influx of wealth can bring you freedom you didn't have before. But it also brings new responsibilities. To handle your inheritance the right way, there are a few things you should know.

COUNTING YOUR CHICKENS

The first step toward being responsible about an inheritance is not to take it for granted before you actually receive it. Even if you're pretty sure that you'll be receiving assets as a result of someone's will, it's a bad idea to spend or invest these assets until you actually have them. After all, if you end up having to wait longer than you expected to receive the

inheritance—or if it loses most of its value while you're waiting—you could find yourself in more debt than you can handle.

If and when you do receive an inheritance you've been expecting, you should still think things over before you act. If you've inherited only a small amount—say, enough for a little vacation—then it can be okay to spend it on whatever it can cover.

But if you're receiving a larger amount, you don't want to waste it. The sudden freedom that comes with a sizeable inheritance makes it easy to spend everything you get without thinking about how the money could benefit you down the road. In fact, you might think about hiring a financial adviser if you receive an inheritance bigger than 5% of your annual income.

Using the adviser of the person who left you money can help you ease into your new financial situation. But don't stick with this person blindly just because you don't want to hurt his or her feelings. Someone who is really going to be able to help you in the long run must suit your needs and your financial style.

INHERITING CASH

If you inherit enough to do something substantial, what should you do with it? Generally, it's best to take a long-term view.

If you have debts—especially credit card debts—your first priority should be to pay them off. In addition to improving your immediate financial situation, you'll be improving your credit rating, which means you'll be able to borrow more easily in the future.

If you're in good standing with lenders, consider using inherited cash to add to your retirement portfolio. You can beef up contributions to your IRA, provided you have earned income. Or you might use part of the inheritance as regular spending money so you can contribute more to your 401(k) or other tax-deferred plan.

INHERITING INVESTMENTS AND PROPERTY

If you inherit investments or property, one of the big questions you'll face is whether to keep what you receive or sell it. Lots of different factors can affect your decision, including the sentimental value of the property, your financial standing at the time, and how well the economy is doing.

One of the biggest concerns is the tax you'll have to pay when you sell the property. The good news is that because of something called a **step up in basis**, you don't have to pay tax on the increased value of inherited assets. When assets are stepped up in basis, they're revalued at the amount they're worth when your benefactor dies, or when his or her estate is valued. So when you sell an inherited asset, you pay taxes as if you had bought it on the date it was valued, not at the time it was actually purchased. You end up saving a lot more money than if you paid based on the increase in value from the date it was purchased.

VALUE $20

STEP UP IN BASIS

VALUE $50

For example, if you buy stock for $20 a share and sell it at $50 a share, your **cost basis**, or original price, would be $20, and you'd pay capital gains taxes on the $30-a-share profit. But if your grandmother buys stock at $20 a share and she dies and leaves it to you when it's valued at $50 a share, your cost basis would be $50. So if you sell it right then at $50 a share, you won't owe any tax. Of course, you could always hold onto it and hope it increases in value. But that means weighing the potential additional gain—or loss—against the immediate cash value you could pocket by selling now.

Planning for Retirement

Smart financial planning can be the difference between the retirement of your dreams and just dreaming about retirement.

Of all the goals you set for yourself, being able to afford a satisfying retirement is one of the biggest and the most important. Everyone says you've got to start preparing by investing, but you've probably got questions: When to start? How much to put away? What to buy?

The good news is, there are answers. You can invest for retirement in two ways: through tax-deferred or tax-free plans and through regular taxable accounts. Ideally, you do both, since each approach can contribute in its own way to providing retirement income. And the sooner you start, the better the odds that you'll accumulate the nest egg you need.

Retirement savings plans that provide tax advantages—whether they let you postpone tax on what you earn or avoid tax entirely on those earnings—are available in several different forms. Some, such as 401(k), 403(b), and 457 plans, are employer sponsored. That means, to contribute, you have to work for an employer who offers a plan. With other plans, such as individual retirement accounts (IRAs), you must earn income or be married to someone who does. Still others, including fixed and variable annuities, let you invest money from any source.

When you invest in taxable accounts—through banks, brokerage firms, mutual fund companies, and other financial institutions—you pay tax on your dividend and interest income every year. But if you ultimately sell your investments for more than you paid, which is one of the goals of investing in the first place, you pay tax on any increase in value at the lower capital gains rate.

THREE: THE MAGIC NUMBER?

Traditionally, financial writers have described the income that you live on during retirement as a three-legged stool: Social Security, your employer sponsored retirement plans, and investments you've made on your own. If one

SHRINKING SOCIAL SECURITY?

No matter what political party is in office, or what their plans are for Social Security, there's almost always talk about what the state of the program will be when today's 20- and 30-year-olds reach retirement age. And since by about 2015 there will be more people collecting benefits than there are people putting money into the system, there's bound to be a change at some point in the future.

Right now Social Security pays for between a third and a half of the average retired worker's monthly income, and somewhat less for those who earned more than the average—currently about $50,000 a year—during their working lives. While it's unlikely that the system will totally disappear, that level of support might shrink, especially for wealthier people. Or the annual cost-of-living increases that the system provides may become smaller across the board. Or the age at which you qualify for full benefits may increase.

The only sure thing about the future of Social Security is that there is *no* sure thing. That's why you can't rely on it too much. And it's why you should make sure you're taking all the steps you can to be sure you'll have a source of retirement income.

of these is reduced or disappears, the other two will have to somehow carry the weight.

While this might seem like a shaky situation, it doesn't have to be if you plan and invest intelligently. After all, while the money you get from Social Security and your retirement plan are both largely linked to how much you make in your working years, there's no set limit to what you can invest, and no restriction on how you invest it. This freedom to move—and grow—makes investing an area where you can make up for ground you might lose elsewhere.

SIDE BY SIDE

If you have the opportunity to put money into a **tax-deferred retirement savings plan** like a 401(k), you can't afford to pass it up. The potential for tax-deferred growth and the chance for matching contributions in employer sponsored plans can do wonders for your nest egg. But these plans aren't the only game in town. Investing on your own can be a great move too.

FACTORS	TAX-DEFERRED PLANS	REGULAR INVESTING
Limits	Annual caps set by federal government and your employer	As much as you can afford
Investing options	Usually limited to what's offered in your employer's plan	Open to whatever is traded on the markets
Employer matching	Optional but often half of what you put in, up to 6% of your salary	None
Current income taxes	None, as your money goes in before taxes are figured	You're investing after-tax money, so there's no tax benefit
Taxes over time	Your earnings compound tax deferred	You pay annual taxes on any interest or dividends
Taxes at withdrawal	Your withdrawals are taxed as regular income	Any gain in value after a year or more is taxed at a lower long-term capital gains rate
Flexibility	You usually can't withdraw before you're 59½ without a 10% penalty	You can sell whenever you want or need to

While it's wise to put as much into a tax-deferred plan as you can—especially when you're focusing on retirement—investing on your own allows you to put more money into different investments. Those investments have the potential to provide a strong return. But, as with all investments, you can lose money.

The IRA Way

An individual retirement account is a sweet deal, so it shouldn't be a hard sell.

Salary reduction plans like 401(k)s are a great way to invest for the future, and if you're eligible to participate in one, you should probably be putting money in.

But what if you don't have access to such a plan right now? Maybe you're freelancing or working for yourself, or your employer doesn't offer a plan. Perhaps you have to wait a year to qualify to participate, and you want to start putting money away sooner. And even if you are part of a plan, you may be looking for a way to invest more than the cap on what you can contribute.

As long as you earn income or are married to someone who does, you can

contribute to an **individual retirement account (IRA)**. There is a cap on what you can invest—$4,000 in 2005, 2006, and 2007. But you don't pay current income tax on any earnings your investments produce and you can trade within the account without owing capital gains tax on any increases in investment value.

OPENING AN ACCOUNT

You can set up an IRA with a bank, a brokerage firm, a mutual fund company, or just about any other financial institution. All you have to do is fill out some simple paperwork and deposit your money.

THE QUALIFYING ROUND

Your first step is figuring out which of the three types of IRAs you qualify to use. The deciding factors are how much you earn and whether or not you're eligible to participate in an employer sponsored plan.

The **traditional deductible IRA**, which allows you to deduct your contribution on your tax return, has the strictest requirements. If you don't have a retirement plan at work, you can deduct all of your contribution. But if you're in a plan, you're more restricted. In 2005, for example, if you're single you can deduct all of your contribution if your **adjusted gross income (AGI)** is $50,000 or less, and decreasing amounts as your income gets closer to $60,000. If you're married, and file a joint return, your combined AGI limits are $70,000 and $80,000. (Those amounts are slated to increase in 2006.)

The **Roth IRA** has qualifying limits, too. You can put all of your contribution in a Roth if you're single and your AGI is $95,000 or less, or if you're married and your combined AGI is $150,000 or less. You can put part of your contribution in a Roth if your AGI is up to $110,000 if you're single or $160,000 if you're married and file a joint return. The balance can go into a **traditional nondeductible IRA**.

Everyone qualifies to open a nondeductible IRA to get the benefit of tax-deferred earnings. True, you're contributing after-tax dollars. But if it's your only IRA option, it's a better choice than no tax-deferred account at all.

BUT WHAT'S BEST?

Figuring out what kind or kinds of IRA you're eligible for doesn't mean you've solved the problem of what kind is best for you. The biggest difference between traditional and Roth IRAs is that traditional IRAs are tax deferred, which means you owe no income tax on any earnings as they accumulate, but you do pay tax when you withdraw. Roth IRAs are tax free, if you follow the rules, so you don't owe tax when you withdraw, though you contribute after-tax income, as you do with a traditional nondeductible IRA.

While everyone's needs are different, you may conclude that the Roth is the best way to go. Since you're investing for the long term, you've got time for your account to grow in value. And it's certainly a bonus not to have to face income taxes later—especially if your tax rate is higher than it is now.

If you don't have a salary reduction plan at work, being able to deduct your contributions to a regular IRA can be smart, since it lets you keep more money in your pocket.

You may want to review your options with a financial adviser or analyze them with the help of an online calculator.

TYPE	PROS	CONS
Roth	• Your earnings grow tax free • You're not required to withdraw at any time	• Your contributions aren't deductible • You must be 59½, and the account open five years to qualify for tax-free status
Traditional nondeductible	• Your earnings grow tax deferred	• Your contributions aren't deductible • You have to pay taxes on withdrawals • You have to start withdrawing at age 70½
Traditional deductible	• Your earnings grow tax deferred • Your contributions are tax deductible	• You have to pay taxes on withdrawals • You have to start withdrawing at age 70½

DOUBLE ADVANTAGE

IRAs provide the best of both worlds in terms of investment vehicles—the flexibility of individual investments combined with the opportunity for tax-deferred growth. So the best IRA investment strategy takes advantage of both these strengths.

DO

Take advantage of the flexibility of IRAs to invest in individual stocks and bonds you can't usually get under a salary reduction plan

Choose investments that have the potential to grow to fund your retirement

Contribute as much as you can early in the calendar year, or at least make regular deposits

DON'T

Make your choices and forget about them because some are sure to be disappointing and should be changed

Focus on tax-free investments like municipal bonds if you've got a traditional IRA, since all earnings will be taxed, and these investments usually don't produce as strong a return as other bonds

Delay until the last possible day (April 15) to make your contribution

Wills and Powers of Attorney

You need will power to be sure your house is in order.

Nobody likes to think about **wills** or other legal documents that deal with what happens to your assets after your death. But unless you think about how your property will be transferred to your family or friends, and how financial decisions will be made if you're not able to deal with them, you risk compounding the grief of your loved ones and beneficiaries.

WHY A WILL?

You might think a will is the last thing you need if you have very few assets to give away.

But even if you're single and struggling to get by that doesn't mean you don't need a will. If you have student loans, mortgage payments, or other debts that your parents have cosigned, making them the beneficiaries of your will allows them to use your assets to pay off what you owe. While they would probably get ownership eventually, it could take more time without a will.

And if you've started a family, you'll definitely want to establish a will to provide for your children. In addition to leaving them your assets, you can use your will to designate a guardian in case something happens to both you and your spouse.

MAKING A WILL

There are three different routes you can take to make a will. They all work, and they're all legal, but one may meet your needs better than the others.

Using a lawyer who specializes in wills and estates is the safest way to go. And if your estate includes any complicated investment holdings—including real estate—or if there's the possibility that someone might challenge your will, it's almost a necessity.

Using a guidebook or a tutorial in a computer program or online can help you write your own will for a fraction of the cost. If you do this, though, think seriously about having a lawyer review the document.

Using a fill-in-the-blanks will is cheap and easy, though the form tends to be generic and pretty inflexible. But if you've got simple wishes for a simple estate—like leaving all of your assets to your spouse or parents—this type of will can be better than no will at all.

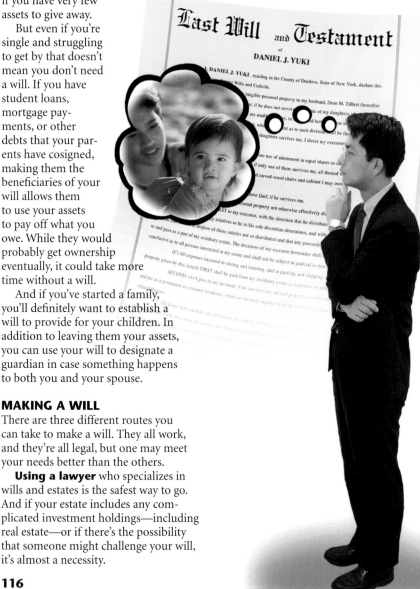

DURABLE POWERS OF ATTORNEY

As long as you have property or an income, you can benefit from having a **durable power of attorney for finances**. You can use this document to designate someone as your **attorney-in-fact**, which ensures that your financial matters will be handled by someone you trust if you're unable to take care of them yourself for any reason.

If your financial situation is pretty simple, you might not think you need that kind of backup. But if you're incapacitated or in the hospital for an extended period of time, you'll need someone to take care of your bills and medical paperwork at the very least.

And then there are larger-scale concerns, like paying taxes and managing investments. If you don't designate someone ahead of time to take care of these matters, the courts will have to do it for you, which can be expensive and potentially uncomfortable for the people involved.

TAKING ACTION

You can create a durable power of attorney that goes into effect as soon as you sign it. Or, if you want it to take effect only if you're incapacitated, you can create what's called a **springing durable power of attorney**. It allows you to control your affairs until you're physically unable to, at which point it springs into effect (hence the name).

All you have to do to create a durable power of attorney is fill out a simple form and sign it in the presence of a notary public. Many stationery and copy stores offer notary public services for a very small fee. Some states require that you have witnesses present at the signing.

Some banks and financial services companies have their own durable power of attorney forms. It's a good idea to see if your bank or brokerage firm requires you to sign these documents to ensure that transactions between the institution and your attorney-in-fact go smoothly. And if you want your attorney-in-fact to deal with any real estate you own, you'll also have to put a copy of the document on file at your local land records office.

If you're married, it's a good idea to give your spouse a durable power of attorney. If you're incapacitated, he or she can use a joint checking account to pay bills, but may not be able sell property you own jointly, and certainly can't do anything with investments, bank accounts, or other property that belongs solely to you.

In fact, it can be useful to have an attorney-in-fact if you're out of the country or out of touch for some other reason and decisions have to be made or documents signed immediately.

POWER OF WHAT?

You don't have to be an attorney to be designated an attorney-in-fact. All the word *attorney* means in this context is someone authorized to act on someone else's behalf.

Take a Tip

If you know a few financial planning tricks, you'll be ahead of the game.

SPECIAL KINDS OF TERM INSURANCE

Many insurance providers offer forms of term life insurance that fit particularly well with young people's needs. For example, **annual renewable term insurance** starts out at a very low price and lets you renew every year for a slightly higher premium.

The low price and short term make it a great way to cover yourself while you're making long-term coverage decisons.

If you're pretty sure you're going to switch from term to whole life in the near future, **convertible term insurance** makes it easy. Once you've qualified for convertible term, you can switch to a whole life policy—or any other type of life insurance—at the same company without having to requalify.

INSURANCE: WHAT NOT TO GET

Not every type of life insurance is a smart bet. Certain types of specialized insurance, which cover you only for particular circumstances, might seem like a great deal because they're usually very cheap. But in the long run, the odds that your family would collect on any of these policies are very small. That means they aren't worth even the tiny price you pay for them. And it's certainly not worth purchasing these policies in place of a traditional term or whole life policy. Take a look at why some of these policies don't pay:

Cancer insurance. As the name suggests, your family doesn't collect unless you die of cancer. So if anything else happens to you, your family won't gain anything.

Accidental death insurance. Accidental death sounds frightening, which can make this type of policy seem like a great idea. But think about it. Conventional insurance covers accidents—and other causes of death.

Credit insurance. Instead of paying your family, this policy pays your creditors. While that might seem like a smart move—especially if you've got a lot of debt— you'll be depriving your loved ones of money they might need if you die.

GETTING TIED IN KNOTS

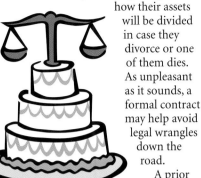

Some couples sign a prenuptial agreement before they marry, spelling out how their assets will be divided in case they divorce or one of them dies. As unpleasant as it sounds, a formal contract may help avoid legal wrangles down the road.

A prior agreement can be essential if you or your spouse has children from a prior relationship, owns a business, or is in line for a large inheritance. It may also be a smart financial move if you are supporting your spouse through a long and expensive education. That way, should you divorce, you may get access to your ex's enhanced earning power.

Each of you should be represented by your own attorney when the agreement is drawn up. And it should be signed well before you tie the knot—not at the midnight hour—if you want the agreement to survive a potential court challenge.

A CAR SHOPPING CALENDAR

You can often get a better deal on a car at the end of the month or the end of a quarter, since there's often competition among salespeople and even among entire dealerships to win high sales awards. Of course, salespeople know that you'll be coming to the lot with that mindset, and if they know you're hot to buy, they won't hesitate to use your eagerness to their own advantage.

One calendar-based car-shopping strategy that might work a little better is to shop toward the end of the year for that year's model, after the coming year's model has already been released. You'll sometimes have a better chance at getting a lower price, since dealers will want to clear old merchandise off their lots.

HEALTHCARE PLANNING

Establishing a durable power of attorney for finances doesn't give your attorney-in-fact the right to make medical decisions on your behalf. But you can establish a **durable power of attorney for healthcare** and designate the same person who is your attorney-in-fact for finances.

If you want to have more control over the medical care you'll receive, you'll probably want to create a **living will**, also known as a **healthcare directive** or a **directive to physicians**. It states the kind of medical treatment you want—and don't want—to receive if you can't communicate your own wishes. Living wills are best known for covering issues like refusing life support, but you can also use them to tell doctors just about anything related to your treatment.

Most professional caregivers opt to prolong life when possible, so if you're opposed to such measures, you should definitely have a living will that states your wishes. And if you do want them to take measures to keep you alive, it never hurts to have one made out anyway. Whatever you do, make sure your family and your doctor know where they can find your living will if they need to.

A few states let you establish a living will and a durable power of attorney on the same form. But in most cases, you'll have to create separate documents if you want to set up both.

The Basics of Investing

Taking the plunge into investing can seem scary, but it doesn't have to be.

Investing is about putting your money to work. If you do it wisely, you can increase your **principal**, or the amount you've invested, over time. The money your investments produce can mean the difference between meeting your financial goals and settling for what you can afford.

Investing isn't the same as saving. When you save, you're putting money in a safe place to earn interest—a bank account, for example. That's fine for building an emergency fund or accumulating money for short-term goals. But your principal won't grow much faster than the rate of **inflation**, or the gradual increase in the prices of goods and services. That can leave you short on buying power.

While there are no guarantees with investing, there is the expectation that over time you'll beat inflation—in some years by a wide margin.

CHARTING A COURSE

At its most basic, investing means buying financial products for **growth**, **income**, or **safety**. You can choose:

- **Stocks** and **mutual funds** that invest in stocks
- **Bonds** and mutual funds that invest in bonds
- **Cash** and **cash equivalent investments**, including certificates of deposit (CDs) and US Treasury bills

Your first step should be to identify a strategy to guide your investment decisions. Unless you've already got a lot of money or investments on hand from an inheritance or a trust fund, you'll be building your investment portfolio from the ground up. So you've got time to learn as you go.

As a start, get a grasp of the basics. Begin with the financial articles in the magazines and newspapers you already read, or look for introductory information in the financial sections of portals and other websites. Talk to friends and family who are already investing.

When you're ready to get serious, it might be a good idea to look for a financial mentor who can help you select specific investments—perhaps a friend or relative who is an experienced investor, or possibly someone at work. It can be a great way to get the encour-

HELPFUL HINTS

There's no hard and fast rule about how much you should be investing, but experts advise aiming for 10% to 15% of your gross income. If you're contributing to a retirement savings plan at work, you can count the percentage you're putting in there as part of your total. And whenever you get a bonus, a gift, or other unexpected cash infusion, it's a good idea to put some or all of it into your investment account as well. That extra boost can make a big difference in what you'll have later on.

INVESTING FOR BEGINNERS

If investing seems like an alien experience, try an experiment. Buy an index fund that tracks a broad segment of the stock market or a highly rated stock mutual fund that's investing for growth. Promise yourself that whatever happens for the next year or two, you won't sell the fund and you won't stop investing in it regularly.

Watch the fund over a period of time so you get used to some ups and downs. Check out what happened to your fund the last time the market tumbled. If you're not prepared, you might panic when the price drops. If you sell, you may have to watch the price go back up again without you.

Each year, evaluate how well your investment has done compared with similar investments. Also consider what you had expected as a return, and what you would have earned if your money were in a savings account.

If the investment is meeting your objectives, hold onto it. If not, sell. By then, you'll be ready to consider your next move—and experienced enough to make it a smart one.

agement you need to make important decisions. And as you expand your investment horizons, your mentor can help you create a strategy for putting together a more diversified portfolio.

START IT UP

You don't need a lot of money to be an investor. But you will need enough cash to buy your first shares of stock or open your first mutual fund. It's smart to set up an investment account so that you can contribute easily and keep track of your progress. A money market account with a brokerage firm or a mutual fund company is one way to go. So is a stock mutual fund. If you've got the account earmarked for investing, you may be less tempted to spend the money on everyday expenses.

Once you have the account set up, decide on an amount you'll contribute every week or month, and stick to it. One idea is to have the money deposited directly from your paycheck or transferred from your checking account. It's even easier than paying a bill—except in this case you're paying yourself.

A LITTLE FUN NOW AND THEN

Investing can be intimidating, and if you've never tried it, it can seem pretty boring as well. But if you give it a little time, chances are you'll come to feel that it's anything but dull. Tracking the performance of companies that interest you, or whose products you use, or even those that make you mad, can be as captivating as following any other part of the news.

After a while, you might find yourself more interested in—and more knowledgeable about—investing and markets than you'd have ever thought possible.

Of course, part of the fun of investing is what it can provide for you later on. If you've got images in your head of a fabulous trip, a dream home, or a leisurely retirement, investing can make them happen. Just remember, there are no guarantees.

A Time and Way to Grow

When you're investing, time has a snowball effect.

If you've heard it once, you've heard it a hundred times: The sooner you start investing, the better. You might hate having to admit that it really is true. But it is.

That's because of **compounding**, a process that lets you make money on your earnings as well as on your principal. Compounding occurs when dividends or interest you earn on your investments are reinvested to form the new base on which future earnings can accumulate. And as that base gets larger, the potential for growth increases.

Here's what can happen over a year:

Base amount on January 1
+Earnings=New base amount
+Earnings=New base amount
+Earnings=New base amount
+Earnings=Value the next January 1

When interest compounds in an insured cash or cash equivalent investment, the dollar value of your account always increases, though it may increase slowly. If you start with $1,000 and you earn 5.25% compounded, you'll have $1,052.50 after a year and 1,107.75 after two years, rather than $1,105. The extra $2.75 is from compounding.

Compounding works a little differently with equity investments such as stocks and mutual funds. In that case, if you reinvest all your earnings to buy additional shares, the number of shares you own increases. But the total value of your account may increase or decrease depending on whether the price per share rises or falls.

For example, suppose you start out with 100 shares of a stock mutual fund valued at $15 a share and reinvest your earnings. By the time you've accumulated 125 shares, the stock market is down and the fund's share price is $12. Despite compounding, your account would be worth the same $1,500 (125 shares x $12 = $1,500).

But, if the stock market gained rather than lost value by the time you'd accumulated 125 shares, and the fund's share price grew to $18 a share, your account value would be $2,250 (125 shares x $18 = $2,250), a 50% increase in value.

And the more shares you accumulate, the more any increase in the share price boosts the value of your investment.

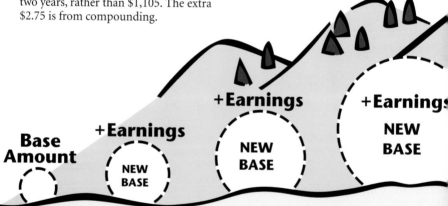

Base Amount **+Earnings** NEW BASE **+Earnings** NEW BASE **+Earnings** NEW BASE

DOLLAR COST AVERAGING

If you want to use volatility to your advantage, **dollar cost averaging** can be a useful investment strategy. When you dollar cost average, you invest the same amount of money in a specific investment on a regular schedule, no matter what the price per share is. For example, you might add $100 to a mutual fund every month.

When the fund's price is up, your $100 buys fewer shares than it does when the price is down. The advantage of continuing to buy through these ups and downs is that if you stick with the plan for an extended period, the average price you pay per share will be less than the actual average share price. But for the strategy to work, you have to buy when prices drop—and putting your money into an investment on the decline can be nerve-wracking, especially if you're not a veteran investor. If you stop buying when prices drop, you'll have paid only the highest prices, and that's exactly what you are trying to avoid.

UPS AND DOWNS, INS AND OUTS

Over the course of a day, a month, or a year, most investment prices fluctuate, sometimes dramatically. They go up and down repeatedly in response to a range of variables from changing market conditions to shifting investor attitudes. This constant movement is known as **volatility**.

Some kinds of investments are more volatile than others. Stocks, for example, tend to change in value more dramatically than bonds or mutual funds. So the shorter the time you plan to own a stock, the more risk you're taking that its price will be down if you need or want to sell it. But short-term volatility doesn't limit the possibility of substantial gain if you hold onto an investment for a long stretch of time.

In contrast, **liquidity** describes the ease and speed with which you can convert an investment into cash with little or no loss in value. Basically, the more liquid an investment is, the less trouble you have selling it for at least the amount you invested. For example, savings accounts and money market funds are considered highly liquid.

Liquidity is especially important if you need money for a financial emergency, or if you're planning to sell the investment at a specific time to meet a particular goal, such as making the down payment on a home or buying a car.

= Total Value

The positive side of putting the same amount of money into an investment every month, no matter how it's doing, is that you get in the habit of investing regularly. That's a good habit to have. And if you're also reinvesting whatever earnings your investment produces, you're getting the added advantage of compounding. But there is one caution: Dollar cost averaging doesn't guarantee you'll make money on your investment or protect you from losses any more than any other investment strategy.

LET IT ROLL

Reinvesting the money your investments may generate is one of the easiest and most reliable ways to take advantage of the power of compounding.

If you invest in a mutual fund, just select the reinvestment option when you open your account. If you invest in stocks, take advantage of stocks that offer **dividend reinvestment plans (DRIPs)**. And if you have money in bonds, put the interest you receive into an investment account to be recycled into the next bond—or other investment—you buy.

You'll still owe income tax on your earnings, at the tax rate that applies, except for the investments you hold in a tax-deferred or tax-exempt retirement account. But your money will go straight to earning more money, rather than sitting around and tempting you to spend it.

Risk and Return

Investing is like life: nothing ventured, nothing gained.

If you want to meet your financial goals, you'll have to learn to live with a certain amount of **risk**. Risk means that as your investments fluctuate in value over time, one or more of your holdings may be worth less than you paid for it. In fact, some investments may turn out to be virtually worthless—or really and truly worthless.

But you have to take some risks to get a significant **return on investment**, sometimes abbreviated as **ROI**. Return includes income you get from an investment, such as dividends or interest, and any **gain**, or profit, from selling the investment for more than you paid to buy it.

For example, say you buy 100 shares of stock for $35 a share, collect a $75 dividend, and sell it for $40 a share. Your return is $575 on the investment: $75 in dividends plus a $500 increase in value (100 shares x $5 increase per share = $500). If you realize that return in one year, your rate of return on the stock would be 16.4% ($575 ÷ $3,500 = .164 or 16.4%).

FINDING YOUR RETURN ON INVESTMENT

	YOU INVEST	YOU SELL
Number of shares	100	100
x Price per share	x $35	x $40
TOTAL	**$3,500**	**$4,000**
Increase (100 x $5)		$500
+ Dividend		+ $75
YOUR RETURN		**$575**
Your return		$575
÷ Amount invested		÷ $3,500
RATE OF RETURN		**16.4%**

That's a pretty good return, especially compared to what you could be earning on the money in a savings account. But that return isn't guaranteed in the next year. In fact, the value of the stock could drop just as easily as it could increase. That's where risk comes in, and why you can lose money when you invest.

Suppose you needed cash when the stock price had dropped to $32 a share. Even if you collect $75 in dividends, you'd lose $225 by selling at the lower price [100 shares x $32 a share = $3,200 sale price – $3,500 purchase price = –$300 + $75 dividends = –$225]. That's a loss of 6.4% on your investment.

NOTHING TO FEAR BUT...

If the idea of risk scares you, get used to it. As an investor you can approach risk in three ways: Embrace it, try to avoid it, or find a way to use risk to your advantage.

You might find risk exhilarating. Taking lots of chances on start-up companies or concentrating on just one or two investments means you'll either make a lot of money or kiss your principal good-bye.

You can try to avoid risk by choosing investments that pose little or no danger to your principal. That includes insured certificates of deposit (CDs). But avoiding what you think of as risk makes you vulnerable to one of the biggest investment risks you face—**inflation**, or the long-term loss of buying power.

By spreading your investments across the range of possibilities, with a small amount in both the safest and the riskiest categories and the bulk in between, you can avoid the greatest risks without giving up the potential for a substantial return. And if you stick to stocks, bonds, and the mutual funds that invest in them, the most you can lose is the amount you invest.

RISKY BUSINESS

Risk has many faces. The sooner you learn to recognize some of the most common ones, and where you're apt to encounter them, the less scary they should be.

Investment risk, sometimes called **business risk**, is the possibility that an investment will not produce the results you expect. For example, suppose two new technologies are introduced at about the same time, both innovative and workable. But only one of the technologies is widely adopted. If you invested in the one that doesn't survive, you may well lose money. But investing in the successful one may produce a substantial return. And if you'd invested in both, your gain in one might offset your loss in the other.

Management risk refers to the possibility that a company's management team may make serious mistakes in directing the company. Whether these errors result from honest miscalculation or from negligence, they can have major financial consequences for the company's stock, resulting in substantial investor losses. On the other hand, superior management can produce outstanding results under certain—though not all—market conditions.

Market risk is the possibility that the equity or bond markets as a whole may drop in value, as may happen in a periodic correction or a more serious recession. In that type of economic climate, the prices of even the most stable investments tend to decline.

No matter how alert you are as an investor, it's difficult to anticipate a market drop. Historically, however, strong markets have always been followed by a period of loss, and the reverse, with weak markets recovering, and growing stronger.

MARKET RISK

ROI

INVESTMENT RISK

MANAGEMENT RISK

START

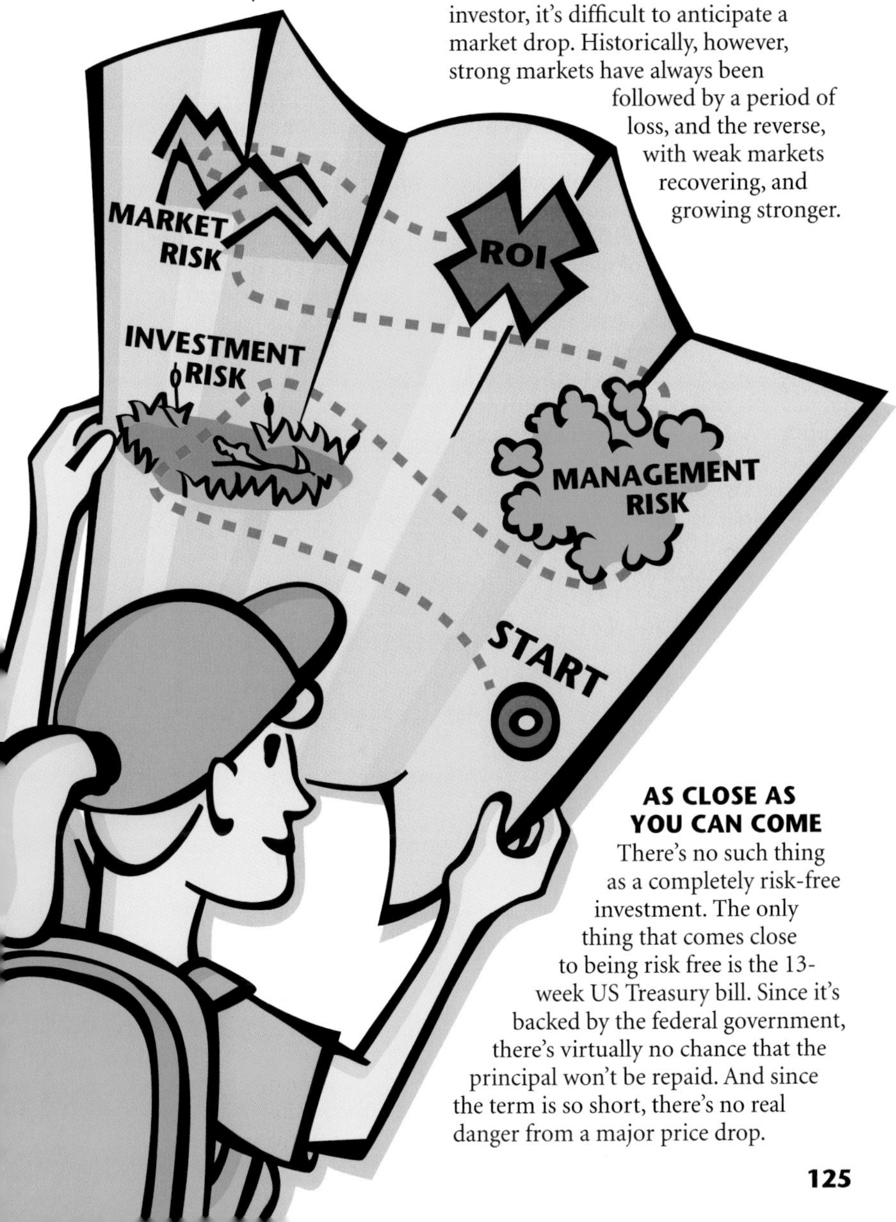

AS CLOSE AS YOU CAN COME
There's no such thing as a completely risk-free investment. The only thing that comes close to being risk free is the 13-week US Treasury bill. Since it's backed by the federal government, there's virtually no chance that the principal won't be repaid. And since the term is so short, there's no real danger from a major price drop.

Allocating Your Assets

If you want your portfolio to grow up big and strong, you've got to feed it the right investments.

How many times did your parents remind you to eat balanced meals so that you'd grow up healthy and strong? When they said balanced, what they had in mind was probably more vegetables and protein and less ice cream and fries.

Well, making smart investment decisions actually works a lot like putting healthy meals together. But with investing, the balanced approach is called **asset allocation**. It means investing a percentage of your investment portfolio in each of the major investment types or **asset classes**: stocks, bonds, and cash.

ASSESSING ASSET CLASSES

One reason to allocate among asset classes is to take advantage of how different classes perform:

1 Each asset class provides strong returns in some years and weak returns in others. For example, large company stocks gained more than 28% in 1998 and another 21% in 1999. But they lost almost 12% of their value in 2001 and another 22% in 2002.

2 The major asset classes tend to shine at opposite times. In years—or periods of years—when stocks provide a strong return, bond returns are often weak. And when stocks falter, bonds often shine. There have also been a few years when you could have earned more by keeping all your money in cash, measured by the return on US Treasury bills, than in either stocks or bonds.

3 You never know which asset class will be strong, or how strong it will be, in any given year or period of years. So the wisest move is to include some of each asset

class in your portfolio. That way, you get the double advantage of benefiting from gains in the asset class or classes that are doing well, and offsetting some weakness in those that are not.

A MATTER OF TASTE

Deciding what percentage of your investment assets to allocate to stocks and stock mutual funds, what percentage to bonds and bond mutual funds, and what percentage to cash and cash equivalents isn't a piece of cake. There's not a single asset allocation that works for everyone. And the allocation that's right for you now probably won't be ideal at every phase of your life.

Your financial goals and your risk tolerance influence the allocations you make. But your age is probably the single most important factor. That's because the element of unpredictability in investing, especially when investing in stocks and stock mutual funds, isn't such a threat

if you've got a long time to reach your goals. But if you're counting on your investment assets to meet a near-term goal, you'll probably want to minimize the risk of losing even some of your principal.

A PLACE TO START

Many financial advisers suggest an easy asset allocation formula: Subtract your age from 100 if you're a man and from 107 if you're a woman. Then allocate a percentage of your portfolio equal to your result to stocks or stock mutual funds. (The extra years recognize that women, on average, live longer than men do.)

That means if you're in your 20s, you'd be investing about 80% of your money in stocks to maximize your potential for long-term growth, with the rest in cash, cash equivalents, or bonds.

By the time you get to be 80, you may want to reduce the percentage you've allocated to stocks to as little as 20% of your portfolio—unless you've already got enough income to live on comfortably. In that case, you might still be investing a substantial portion of your portfolio for growth (and the benefit of your heirs).

Remember, though, that while a carefully allocated portfolio can increase your long-term return and help offset current losses, it can't guarantee that you won't lose money on individual investments or come out short in realizing your goals.

CHANGING THE MIX

Investment values shift over time, so that an asset class that initially made up 25% of your portfolio might, at some point, increase to 40% while another asset class may shrink from 25% to 10%.

For example, investors who had lots of money in small, high-tech companies in 1998 watched the value of those investments balloon in 1999 to a disproportionately large percentage of their portfolios. Yet, when these stocks plummeted in 2000, holdings in these small companies represented a substantially smaller percentage of their diminished portfolios in 2001.

If your goals and your risk tolerance haven't changed, and the allocation model you started with still seems right, you might want to reallocate your investments from time to time to make sure that your actual portfolio is in line with the portfolio you intend to own.

To make that happen, you might sell some of the investments that have increased in value to buy investments in the asset class that has lost value. Or you might put any new money you're investing into the currently underperforming asset class.

But that's not something you need to worry about every day. Many financial advisers suggest that it's enough to review and reallocate your portfolio once a year. Others suggest that you can ignore imbalances unless the value of any class exceeds the allocation you originally selected by 15% or more.

Investing in Stocks

The stock market has its ups and downs, but it can be a good ride.

When you invest in a stock, you're buying part of a publicly traded company. That piece, also known as your **equity** or ownership share in the company, means you're in a position to profit from the company's success—or lose money if its share price drops and you sell.

Despite the potential risk involved, stocks are one of the most popular types of investments, especially for long-term goals. It's for good reason: They've historically provided better returns than any other kind of investment—almost twice as much as long-term government bonds and about two and a half times as much as cash since year-end 1925, according to Ibbotson Associates.

CREATING A PORTFOLIO

Suppose, for example, that price were no object and you could create an instant portfolio of six stocks. There are some basic principles you'd want to keep in mind to be sure that your porfolio turned out to be diversified.

Be sure that each of the stocks is from a different sector of the economy. You may want to avoid the sector your employer is in, or limit yourself to one company in that sector, so that you aren't depending on one industry for investment gains *and* your paycheck.

UPS AND DOWNS

A stock doesn't have a fixed value the way some other investments do. What it's worth can go as high as you and other investors are willing to pay to own it—usually because you expect it to be worth even more in the future. But it can also drop in value, sometimes to almost nothing, if the company that issued it isn't meeting investor expectations, or is part of an industry that's out of favor with investors, or if the market as a whole tumbles.

Historically, investors have picked companies based on how strong their earnings were and how consistently those earnings increased. But in the late 1990s, many technology and Internet stocks increased rapidly in value even though those companies weren't making money. Some commentators speculated that a new era in investing had arrived. But that phase was soon being described as a bubble doomed to burst, and investors went back to looking at earnings.

FINDING YOUR STYLE

Investing in stocks is a matter of style. If you're a **buy and hold** investor, you're in for the long haul. You buy stocks you think will increase in value over time, and you hold onto them—even through price drops and down markets.

You may even buy more shares when the stock loses value, since you'll pay less per share than when the price is high. And if, from time to time, the price goes high enough and the stock **splits**, you end up with even more shares.

If you **trade**, you buy stocks you expect to increase enough in value in the short term so that you can sell them for a profit. With this approach, you may want to set some guidelines for when you should sell. For example, you might decide you'll sell any stock whose price has increased 20% and reinvest in another promising stock.

If you concentrate on companies that show promise of future growth, be sure to include at least one or two well-established companies, even if their growth rate is likely to be slower.

If the stocks that interest you have P/Es that are higher than the current average, you might look for one or two under-valued companies that show promise of long-term growth. You can find P/E figures in the stock pages of the news-paper or on financial or company websites.

Consider dividing your portfolio evenly among **large-cap** stocks (with market caps over $10 billion), **mid-cap** stocks (with market caps between $2 and $10 billion) and **small-cap** stocks (with market caps below $2 billion).

Remember, though, that long-term gains on stocks you own more than a year are taxed at a much lower rate than short-term gains.

SIZING UP STOCKS

If you're investing in stocks, it's a good idea to **diversify** your portfolio. That means building a portfolio of stocks that tend to react differently to changes in the economy, to grow in value at different rates, and to carry different levels of risk.

To evaluate how diversified your portfolio is, and to identify the kind of stock you might buy next, you can classify stocks and the companies that issue them in several ways:

- By **sector**, or industry
- By **growth** potential, which is a stock's apparent capacity to increase in price
- By **valuation,** to assess whether a stock's current price is higher or lower than the company's financial standing and growth potential seem to deserve

P/E RATIOS

Investors often use a stock's **price-to-earnings ratio (P/E)** to get a sense of its value in relation to other stocks in the same sector or in the market at large.

A P/E—which you find by dividing the current price per share by the company's earnings per share—that's much higher than the market average may be a warning that investors expect a higher return from the stock than it may be able to deliver. And a lower than average P/E may indicate either a company in trouble or one poised to produce a good return on investment.

- By **market capitalization**, or market cap for short, which is the price of one share of stock multiplied by the total number of existing shares

129

Investing in Bonds

Bonds can help balance your portfolio.

Bonds are **debt investments**. When you buy a bond, you're really lending money, or **principal**, to a company or government for a certain **term**, or period of time. The company or government—known as the **issuer**—promises to pay you interest on the principal, just as you would have to pay **interest** if you borrowed money from a bank. And when the bond matures at the end of its term, you're promised the principal back.

YOU INVEST IN BONDS

CORPORATE BOND · US TREASURY BOND · MUNICIPAL BOND · AGENCY BOND

TYPES OF BONDS

Corporate bonds are issued by public companies to raise money for various purposes, from expansion to modernization. In general, these bonds pay higher interest than other bonds, but that interest is taxable unless you buy the bonds through a tax-deferred or tax-exempt retirement savings plan.

US Treasury bills, notes, and bonds are issued by the federal government to raise money for running the country. Since they're backed by the government's ability to levy taxes rather than just by corporate profits, these bonds are somewhat less risky—and tend to pay somewhat lower interest—than corporate bonds. You have to pay federal income taxes on the interest, but not state or local taxes.

BONDS < **YOU CAN REINVEST**

FOR WHAT IT'S WORTH

A bond's **par value** is the amount that you lend the issuer and the amount that you get repaid at maturity. In most cases, par value is $1,000. But various market forces and investor attitudes can change bond prices just as they change stock prices. The only difference is that with bonds, these increases and decreases are always in relation to par value.

What happens to interest rates has the biggest single impact on what bonds are worth. As rates go up, the prices of existing bonds go down because they provide comparatively less income. For example, if interest rates increase from 5% to 6%, you'd get $10 more income per $1,000 investment on a new bond than on an existing bond. As a result, an older bond becomes less attractive to investors than a newer, higher-paying one, and its market price will drop below $1,000. When a bond sells below par, it is selling **at a discount**.

Similarly, if the interest rate drops, existing bonds paying the older, higher rate become more desirable because they provide more income. In that case, investors will pay more than $1,000, or what's known as a **premium**, to own them.

Municipal bonds, often known as **munis**, are issued by state and local governments to raise money for various projects and expenses. Most municipal bond interest is free of federal income tax. And if you buy munis from the state where you live, the interest you earn is tax free. But if you buy munis issued by another state, you have to pay state and local taxes on the interest.

Agency bonds are issued by various government agencies for specific projects. For example, **Ginnie Mae**, the **Government National Mortgage Association**, issues bonds to help finance affordable mortgages. Agency bonds tend to pay slightly higher interest than other government bonds because they pose a marginally higher risk. But you don't get the tax breaks you do with Treasurys or munis. The interest these bonds pay is usually taxable on all levels.

CLIPPING COUPONS

Zero-coupon bonds, sometimes called **zeros**, work a little differently than most other bonds. You buy them at a **deep discount**, for a price way below their par value. For example, you might pay $11,000 for a $20,000 zero-coupon bond. You don't receive any interest during the bond's term, but when it reaches maturity you get the face value plus all the interest that accumulates over the years.

If you're investing for a particular goal with a predictable time frame—a child's college education, for example—the relatively low cost and big payout of zeros can make them a smart move.

But if you're just starting to invest and you don't have a definite goal for this portion of your investment portfolio, zeros may not be smart. You'd be tying up a lot of money for a long time, or risking a loss if you sell, since zero-coupon prices are volatile. And even though you don't get any interest until the bond matures, you still have to pay taxes on it each year.

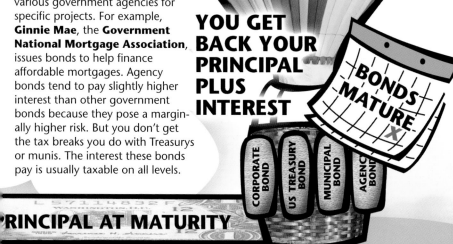

YOU GET BACK YOUR PRINCIPAL PLUS INTEREST

PRINCIPAL AT MATURITY

BUYING TO HOLD

If you buy a bond when it's issued and hold onto it until it matures, it's one of the most straightforward investments you can make. You pay your money up front, and you know beforehand exactly how much you're going to earn, and when you'll get your principal back. This simplicity makes it a favorite with traditional investors.

Of course, investing this way makes you vulnerable to inflation. Since the interest a bond pays is usually fixed—the one exception is inflation-indexed Treasury bonds—the amount you receive over time will buy less and less as time goes on. This becomes a particularly pressing problem with long-term bonds, which is one of the reasons they typically pay a higher rate than short-term bonds. After all, there's got to be some incentive for tying up your money.

BUYING TO TRADE

You can also trade bonds actively through a broker on the **secondary market**. That means buying bonds that another investor is selling—or selling the bonds you own because there are investors who want to buy. Some investors regularly buy and sell bonds as they do stocks, trying to make money on price fluctuations and interest rate changes.

131

Mutual Funds and ETFs

Pooling your money with other investors can bring swimming results.

When you invest in a **mutual fund**, your money gets combined with the money of the fund's other investors. A professional **manager** decides how to invest those assets based on the fund's **investment objective**, what's happening in the financial markets, and his or her **investment style**, or approach to choosing what to buy and when to sell.

An investment objective describes the financial results the fund aims to deliver. For example, one fund's objective may be long-term **price appreciation**, or growth in value, while another fund may invest to produce a combination of current income and long-term growth.

FUND FACTS

Mutual funds come in three basic varieties: **stock funds**, **bond funds**, and **money market funds**.

Stock funds invest primarily in stocks, though the stocks they buy vary from fund to fund. Most stock funds invest primarily for growth, but some, called growth and income funds or equity income funds, invest for current income as well by buying dividend-paying stocks.

Since most stock funds invest in dozens of companies, they're by nature **diversified** investments. Weak performances by some stocks that the fund owns can be offset by strong performances from others. That makes the fund more price-stable overall than individual stocks. However, if the stock market as a whole drops in value, the value of most funds invested in the market will drop as well.

Bond funds buy bonds. Investing in a bond fund provides current income, just as investing in individual bonds does. But you can invest smaller amounts and get greater diversification by buying shares in a fund. And you can automatically reinvest your income to buy more shares in the fund, something you can't do with individual bonds.

But bond funds aren't bonds. Your shares in a bond fund don't mature at a particular time, they don't earn a fixed rate of interest, and there's no promise that you'll get your original investment back. Instead, the value of bond fund shares goes up and down to reflect the changing values of its bonds in the secondary market.

INVESTORS

FUND COMPANY

Money market funds invest in short-term bonds and other debt investments, with the goal of maintaining a share price of $1 per share. These funds pay interest, usually at about the same rate as short-term CDs. And while they're not federally insured, they've generally been considered safe.

A money market fund can work as a parking place for your investment account, as your emergency fund, and, with most funds, as a checking account, though there may be a minimum of $500 per check. But when interest rates are low, the fund may pay little or nothing.

MARKET PRICES

A mutual fund's **value**, or price per share, is based on the value of its **underlying investments**, which are the stocks or bonds it owns, and the number of shares it has issued. To find the fund's **net asset value** (**NAV**), or the market value of one share of the fund, you divide the total combined value of its underlying investments, minus fund expenses, by the number of existing shares.

Both the underlying value and the number of shares change all the time. So each fund computes its NAV at the end of every business day. You can find this information in newspapers and online.

If you buy shares in a fund directly from the investment company that offers the fund for sale, you usually don't pay a sales commission, or **load**. If you buy through your financial adviser, your

EXCHANGE TRADED FUNDS

Another approach to pooled investing is buying shares of exchange traded funds (ETFs). Each ETF tracks a particular market index, such as the Standard & Poor's 500 (S&P 500) and is listed on a stock market, where it trades throughout the day. The price moves up and down to reflect supply and demand, though it never varies significantly from the fund's NAV.

ETFs tend to cost less to own than actively managed stock and bond funds and even some index mutual funds, a cost that's calculated as an **expense ratio**. But you usually pay a commission to buy and sell, as you do when you trade stocks.

Another potential advantage is that you may have fewer short-term capital gains than you do with a mutual fund. One reason is that ETFs are not trying to beat the market, so their portfolios tend to change only when the underlying indexes change.

Some investors use ETFs to achieve greater diversification at lower cost than they could by buying individual investments, but, of course, ETFs can lose value in a flat or falling market.

broker, or another intermediary, you generally do pay a load, either when you buy (in the case of Class A shares), or when you sell your shares (Class B shares), or every year you own the fund (Class C shares).

TWO WAYS TO GET PAID

Mutual funds pay out their profits to their shareholders each year. **Income distributions** are paid from the dividends or interest the fund earns on its investments. **Capital gains distributions** are paid from any profits the fund makes by selling investments it owns.

You can take these distributions in cash or you can reinvest them to buy more shares in the fund. Reinvesting is an easy way to buy more shares, and can help build the value of your account.

There is one catch: You owe some tax on your distributions every year even if you reinvest. The only exception is if you own the fund through a 401(k) plan, IRA, or another tax-deferred account.

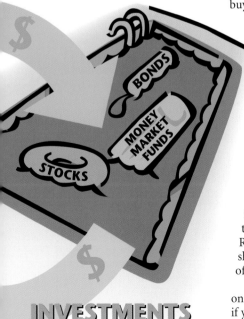

INVESTMENTS

Getting More Investing Power

Stocks, bonds, and cash are your main fuel source. But other investments can give you a boost.

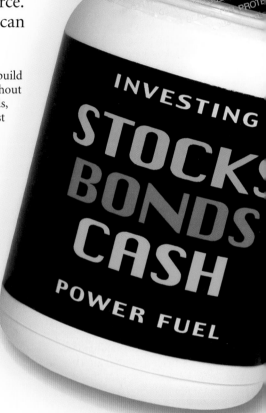

While it's completely possible to build a strong investment portfolio without looking further than stocks, bonds, and cash—or the funds that invest in them—there's a range of other investment opportunities that can help you achieve your financial goals.

Some choices, like **real estate** or **collectibles**, have the added advantage of giving you something tangible to enjoy while you're investing.

Others, such as options, futures contracts, start-up companies, or companies that aren't publicly traded, are higher-risk choices that you may not be ready to consider just yet—or that you may not yet qualify to get involved in.

THE REAL (ESTATE) DEAL

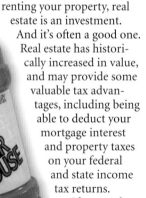

Whether you're living in property you own or living off money you make from renting your property, real estate is an investment. And it's often a good one. Real estate has historically increased in value, and may provide some valuable tax advantages, including being able to deduct your mortgage interest and property taxes on your federal and state income tax returns.

If you make a profit on the sale of your home, there's another break. If you've lived there for at least two of the five years before you sell, you don't have to pay any capital gains tax on up to $250,000 of your profit if you're single, or up to $500,000 if you're married and file a joint return.

Of course, there's no guarantee you'll make money in real estate. And you could have a harder time selling at a profit than with other types of investments. That's because real estate is **illiquid**, which means it can take time to convert your investment to cash, especially if you try to sell during periods of high mortgage rates or limited demand. And you may have to settle for less than you paid if you need to sell at a certain time.

If you don't want to lay out all the money necessary to invest in actual property, you can buy shares in publicly traded **Real Estate Investment Trusts (REITs)**, which invest pools of money in a variety of real-estate ventures. Of course, REITs have risks as well, but they offer you the safety of greater diversification than you could get from buying property on your own.

A MATTER OF TASTE... FOR A PRICE

Collectibles include objects like fine art, antiques, stamps, coins, toys, fine wine, rare books or music, and basically any other possession that people consider valuable.

Focusing on collectibles can make investing a lot of fun, and you can make a good deal of money if you have an eye for what will be hot in the future.

But unlike publicly traded securities or mutual funds, for which there are organized and efficient markets, there's no guarantee that anyone will want to buy what you have when you want—or need—to sell it. This uncertainty means there's no way to anticipate the level of return this type of investing may provide.

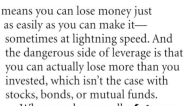

PRECIOUS METALS

Precious metals like gold, silver, platinum, and palladium can add enduring value to your portfolio, although their market prices vary drastically with supply and demand. If you're just getting into investing, it can be risky to own metals directly by buying actual gold bars or certificates that represent ownership from banks or other institutions. Buying stock in mining companies—or better yet, shares in mutual funds that invest in these companies—can give you a little more liquidity and diversification.

ONE STEP REMOVED

A **derivative** is an investment, such as an option or a futures contract, whose value depends on the value of an **underlying investment**, such as a stock or **commodity**. (Commodities are the raw materials in consumer products, such as wheat or crude oil.)

Derivatives can be attractive because they allow you to use **leverage** to invest without laying out a lot of money. But derivative prices are volatile, which means you can lose money just as easily as you can make it—sometimes at lightning speed. And the dangerous side of leverage is that you can actually lose more than you invested, which isn't the case with stocks, bonds, or mutual funds.

When you buy or sell a **futures contract**, you're agreeing to buy or sell a specific amount of the underlying investment by the **expiration date** on that contract. But since there's no guarantee that you'll make money on the transaction, what most investors do is buy an offsetting contract as well—for example, one that requires them to sell if their original contract requires them to buy—hoping to make money on the changing value of the contracts.

When you buy an **option**, you pay a **premium** for the right to buy or sell a specific amount of the underlying investment at a predetermined price, known as the **strike** or **exercise price**, within a particular time frame. Unlike a futures contract, which you're required to settle, you're not obligated to do anything if you buy an option. You can just let it expire, so your only cost is the premium you paid for the right to buy.

But an option can be an opportunity to profit if you've anticipated correctly how the underlying investment is going to change in value and if you buy or sell accordingly.

If you sell an option, you collect the premium, but you're obligated to buy or sell the underlying investment at the strike price if the option buyer exercises the option. That could mean losing money, possibly more than you made on the premium. For example, one risk is selling an option on stock you don't own. If the option is exercised, you have to buy enough shares at the market price to meet your obligation to sell. That could cost you a bundle.

Online Investing

On the Web, investing is just a click away.

With access to financial and news websites, you can get free, up-to-the-minute information on stock and bond markets and real-time quotes on individual investments from anywhere at any time.

Basic screens on most sites show the major indexes, the latest trading prices, plus the kinds of information you can find in newspapers, financial magazines, annual reports, and prospectuses. There may also be links to research about individual investments.

Many sites let you identify topics you want to follow and have that news delivered to you on the site's homepage, a personalized homepage, or by email. And if you open an online brokerage or mutual fund account, you can act on your investment decisions by trading on the site.

OPENING AN ACCOUNT

Opening an online trading account begins with filling out an application you'll find on the brokerage firm's website. US brokerage firms require a Social Security number for US citizens and residents and an IRS Form W-8 for international investors. They ask about

INFORMATION OVERLOAD

The drawback of having so much information available is that it can be hard to put it into perspective. Minute-by-minute fluctuations in the markets can be intimidating, and maybe even a little frightening, especially if you're not an experienced investor. So keep in mind that not every event in the business world, even those involving companies whose stock or bonds you own, will have an impact on your portfolio, especially over the long term.

your work, your income, and your investment experience. They may also ask for a financial reference.

You can apply to open individual or joint online trading accounts, as well as specialized accounts for retirement or education savings. When the account is

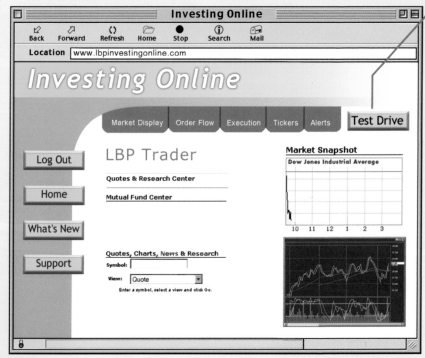

open—often within 24 hours of your application being approved—you can start trading. As with other US brokerage accounts, you have to pay for stock and bond purchases within a fixed period from the date of the trade execution. When it's three days, the settlement date is described as **T+3**, and when it's one day the settlement date is **T+1**. If payment isn't received, the transaction isn't settled.

You can handle those payments by transferring money from a money market or margin account you've set up with the firm, by check, or by electronic transfer.

NOT PLAYING FOR KEEPS

You can test your research skills and your investment strategy by creating a mock stock portfolio—a feature that many online financial sites offer. All you have to do is follow the directions on the site for setting up the hypothetical account. Then you can choose investments and track their performance without actually putting any of your money at risk.

TRADING SAVINGS

There's a financial benefit to investing online: It usually costs less.

Unlike most traditional brokerage firms, which charge a commission based on the size of your stock trade or an annual fee based on the value of your portfolio, many online firms charge a fixed rate for any trade up to 1,000 shares, regardless of the price per share.

For example, if you buy 500 shares at $65 a share, a transaction of $32,500, you may not pay more than $30 for the online transaction. With a traditional full-service broker, however, you might be charged between $325 and $650—or 1% to 2% of the value of the trade—for the same transaction.

Discount brokerage firms, while less expensive than full-service firms, also tend to base their commissions on the amount of the transaction.

What you give up by trading online is the chance to interact with an investment professional who, in addition to carrying out your buy and sell orders, has an ethical responsibility to alert you to potentially unwise decisions.

NOT ALWAYS QUICK ENOUGH

Online brokerage firms also make trading more convenient. In most cases, buy and sell instructions you type into your computer during regular trading hours are confirmed almost immediately. That's generally the case with phone calls to your broker as well.

But as fast as trading over the Web is, speed isn't guaranteed. Sometimes—especially when volume is high and you're eager to buy or sell at a certain price—the electronic systems that support online trading can have trouble keeping up.

And while not common, there have been occasional glitches on most online sites that shut down trading for a period of time.

But online trading does have a time-related advantage. If you place an order online while the markets are closed, it should be automatically executed the next day. You don't have that convenience with phone orders.

TRADING BY DAY

One potentially dangerous consequence of online trading is getting involved in **daytrading**, or buying and selling investments rapidly, often within a matter of minutes, to take advantage of quick price changes.

The problem with daytrading is that it's impossible to predict how much or how fast prices will change. Plus, if you're buying and selling at lightning speed, you're piling up trading costs. In fact, most individual daytraders end up losing money.

...AND BY NIGHT

After-hours trading, which occurs during certain hours when traditional exchanges are closed, is increasingly open to individual investors. But some online brokerage firms charge extra for after-hours transactions. And since trading volume is lower during these times, it can be harder to find good prices. You may decide that it's smarter to wait and place your electronic order for execution when the markets open again.

The Words on the Street

If you want to walk the walk in the world of investing, it helps to be able to talk the talk.

CAPITAL GAINS

When you make money by selling an asset, your profit is known as a **capital gain**. For example, say you buy 100 shares of stock at $20 a share and then sell at $22 a share. You'd have a capital gain of $2 a share, for an overall gain of $200.

If you've owned the asset for less than a year when you sell it, you have a **short-term capital gain**. If it's been longer than a year, it's a **long-term capital gain**. The good thing about holding onto stock until your capital gains become long term is that they're taxed at a much lower rate than other income—only 15% if your marginal tax rate is 25% or higher, and only 5% if it's 15% or lower. That means investing for the long run can be tax-savvy as well as just plain smart.

If you lose money on an investment, you have a capital loss. You can subtract these losses from your gains before figuring the tax you owe.

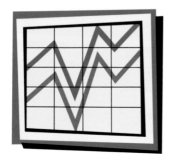

INDEXES

Indexes track changes in a specific financial market or markets, usually expressing these changes as percentages of a total point value. Each index tracks its market or markets from a different starting point, which can be anywhere from the previous day to many years ago. This, and the fact that indexes include different investments from within the same market, are among the reasons why each index reports different results for the same time period.

Index funds allow you to invest in the performance of a major stock or bond index. Since these mutual funds invest in all of the securities included in the index, they go up and down in value along with the index. Investing in an index fund can be a smart move in a bull market, since the index's rising prices will raise the fund's value. But during an economic downturn, a more actively managed fund might be able to seek out good opportunities that an index fund would miss—or avoid the dogs that an index has to include.

DIVIDENDS

The **dividends** you earn on most US stocks and some international stocks are considered qualified, and are taxed at the same federal rate as your long-term capital gains, or a maximum of 15%. That's not the case with interest income, dividends paid on real estate investment trusts (REITs), or collectibles.

That may be an incentive to include stocks in your taxable investment portfolios and emphasize other types of investments in your tax-deferred accounts. Withdrawals from those accounts are taxed at your regular income tax rate.

Not all profitable companies pay dividends, though, preferring to reinvest in the company, make acquisitions, or buy back shares.

TOTAL RETURN

When you're investing for growth, calculating an investment's **total return** is the best way to judge how well it's doing. To find return, add an investment's change in value to any earnings it provides. For example, if you bought $2,000 worth of stock that's now worth $2,150, and it paid you a $50 in dividends, your total return would be $200 ($150 + $50).

Change in value
\+ Earnings
=TOTAL RETURN

To help compare return on investments of different sizes, you can figure the **percent return**, which is the return divided by the original price of the investment. So in the example above, your percent return would be 10%, or $200 ÷ $2,000.

YIELD

If you want to measure what you're actually making on an investment, find its **yield**. Yield is an investment's dividends or interest payments divided by the original amount you invested. So if you earned $50 a year on a $1,000 bond, your yield would be 5% ($50 ÷ $1,000). Similarly, you find **current yield** by dividing your annual income from the investment by its current market price.

Yield can be a good way to evaluate an income-bearing investment like a bond or money market fund. But for other types of investments, it doesn't provide as complete a picture as total return does.

INVESTMENT STYLES

If your image of investing is a roller-coaster ride of big gains and equally big losses in rapid, heart-stopping succession, you're mistaking one tiny segment of the investing community for all investors. In fact, there are almost as many approaches to investing—sometimes called **investment styles**—as there are people who invest.

In broad terms, investors are generally described as **conservative, moderate,** or **aggressive**.

Conservative investors are primarily concerned with safeguarding the assets they already have. While they may choose some investments they expect to grow in value, they try to minimize the chance of losing any **principal**, or the amount they've invested.

Moderate investors seek growth and some income from a substantial portion of their portfolio, while investing a smaller percentage to protect their principal and a smaller percentage still on speculative investments.

Aggressive investors concentrate on investments with the potential for significant growth provided by high-risk investments, although they run a greater chance of losing some or all of their principal.

Your approach to investing may be a combination of these three styles. For example, you might invest some of your portfolio conservatively, most of it moderately, and a small portion aggressively.

That combination is sometimes described as an investment pyramid—a base of safety, a main structure of moderation, and a cap of risk.

AGGRESSIVE

MODERATE

CONSERVATIVE

139

Getting a Grip on Taxes

Taxes put a squeeze on your spendable income.

Taxes are hard to love. Income taxes in particular are complicated, and they cost you money. But since there's no good way to avoid them, it helps to understand how you can pay the government as little as possible of your earned and unearned income without running into trouble with the law.

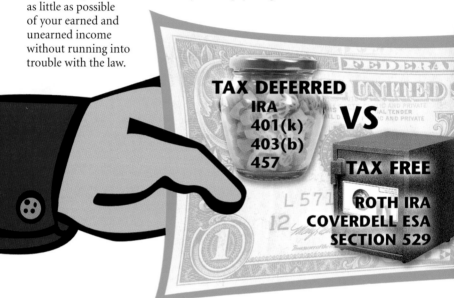

TAX DEFERRED
IRA
401(k)
403(b)
457

VS

TAX FREE
ROTH IRA
COVERDELL ESA
SECTION 529

TAXING TERMS

One of the best ways to reduce your tax bill is by taking advantage of the incentives the federal government offers to encourage you to invest. That includes opening **tax-deferred accounts** or making **tax-free investments**.

Tax deferred means that you can postpone paying taxes on investment earnings and sometimes on investment principal as well. But that advantage applies only to investments you make in special tax-deferred retirement accounts, such as traditional individual retirement accounts (IRAs) and employer sponsored retirement savings plans, such as 401(k), 403(b), or 457 plans. In fact, no income tax is due on a tax-deferred account until you withdraw money. Then, tax is due in the year you withdraw.

In contrast, earnings on tax-free investments are never taxed, though you do have to pay income tax on the money you invest. Investments that are federally tax free (or, more accurately, tax exempt) include Roth IRAs, Coverdell ESAs, and Section 529 plans, which let you save for children's college expenses, and municipal bonds issued by state and local governments. In addition, federal government bonds are free from state and local, but not federal, income taxes.

THINKING AHEAD

If you earn money, buy a house, get married, have children, start a business, save for retirement, or make an investment, it will affect the amount of the federal income tax you owe.

Tax planning is one way to make the tax system work for you instead of against you. Basic tax planning involves two steps:

- Recognizing the tax consequences of your financial decisions
- Making choices that will reduce or postpone the tax you owe

For example, if you sell an investment that has increased in value to give you cash to buy a new car, you'll have a capital gain on your profit. That will increase your tax bill. To offset this gain, you might want to sell investments that have lost value. That way, you may be able to deduct your capital losses from your capital gain to reduce or eliminate the amount on which you owe tax.

GETTING THE TIMING RIGHT

There are deadlines that govern the actions you can take to reduce your taxes. With the exception of contributions to tax-deductible IRAs or to certain other retirement plans, which you can usually make as late as April 15 for the previous year, you have to complete all of your transactions by December 31 of the year for which the taxes are due.

As essential as tax planning is, there's an important caution. You don't want to make financial decisions solely because they would reduce your taxes. For example, even though the interest on municipal bonds is tax free that doesn't mean they are a better investment for you than stocks.

IS THIS PROGRESS?
The US income tax system is **progressive**, which means that people with higher incomes are taxed at higher rates than those with lower incomes are. The argument in favor of this approach is that the greatest tax burden falls on those who can afford to carry it. Opponents argue that it imposes an unfair burden on the people

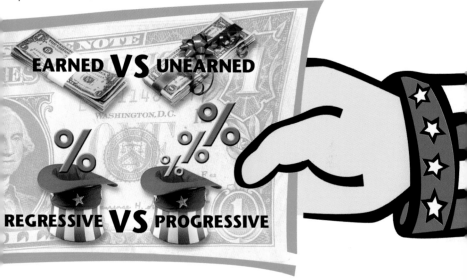

HOW THE TAX SYSTEM WORKS
The federal government, most state governments, and some local governments tax your wages and other **earned income**, as well as your income from investments, or **unearned income**, to get the money they need to keep running. And they collect most of those taxes through **withholding**.

Withholding means your employer holds back part of your gross pay, reducing what you get to take home, and sends that withheld amount to the correct government agency—to the **Internal Revenue Service (IRS)** for federal taxes and to state or local agencies that levy taxes. By having some tax withheld from each paycheck, you pay all or most of the income tax you owe by the end of the tax year.

Income taxes aren't the only money that's withheld. Your employer must also withhold money for Social Security and Medicare, as required by the **Federal Insurance Contributions Act (FICA)**. And you can choose to have your contributions to employer sponsored retirement savings plans, payments for health insurance, and other expenses withheld as well.

whose ingenuity and hard work make the economy strong.

A different system, which taxes everyone at the same rate, as sales taxes do, is called a **regressive**, or flat, tax. Advocates of a flat income tax argue that it's simpler and does away with the kinds of tax breaks that tend to favor the wealthy. But opponents say that a flat tax means the middle class would carry too large a proportion of the total tax bill.

THE CHAIN OF COMMAND
Taxes don't just happen. Congress passes the federal tax laws that make up the Internal Revenue Code (IRC), sets the tax rates, and authorizes the way tax money is spent. The Internal Revenue Service (IRS), which is part of the US Department of the Treasury, interprets the Code through a series of regulations and collects the taxes.

The Rating Game

It may not feel like a match made in heaven, but what you pay in income taxes goes hand in hand with what you earn and who you are.

You pay federal income tax at one or more **tax rates**, or percentages of your taxable income. That's because the government slices income into graduated ranges, or segments, called **tax brackets**, with each bracket taxed at an increasingly higher rate. For single filers in tax year 2005, taxable income up to $7,300 was in one bracket, income between $7,300 and $29,700 in the next highest bracket, and so on. The top bracket included taxable income over $326,450.

If your total taxable income falls within the bracket

Tell me about your tax rate

The Rating Game

AT THE MARGIN

Your **marginal tax rate** is the highest rate at which you pay income tax. Sometimes it's described as the rate you pay on your last dollar of income.

People with the lowest taxable incomes have a marginal rate of 10% and those with the highest have a marginal rate of 35%. But unless you pay at just the 10% rate, your **effective tax rate**, or the actual percentage of your total taxable income that you pay, is always less than your marginal rate.

For example, if you were single in tax year 2005, you paid $15,507 on a taxable income of $75,000. Your marginal rate was 28% but your effective rate was just under 21% ($15,507 ÷ $75,000 = 20.68%).

I pay tax at all six rates!

35%

I know how to get the greatest tax advantage

33%

I just paid $15,746 on a taxable income of $75,000

28%

I've got large tax benefits

25%

Let's file jointly!

15%

I pay the lowest marginal tax rate

10%

Rates for 2002 and 2003

STATE AND LOCAL TAXES

While federal income taxes get the most attention, you may also be paying income taxes to the state where you live. Just seven states collect no income tax at all—Alaska, Florida, Nevada, South Dakota, Texas, Washington, and Wyoming. Two others—New Hampshire and Tennessee—tax interest and dividend income but not earned income.

While state income tax rates tend to be significantly lower than federal rates, you may be in for a shock when you add the two together to find what's known as your combined tax rate. If you live in a city that also collects income tax, the bite can be even larger.

While you can deduct certain taxes you pay to your state and city on your federal return if you itemize your deductions, about the only way to avoid local taxes is to relocate to a state that doesn't impose them.

taxed at the lowest rate, you pay at that one rate. But if you have taxable income that puts you into the next higher bracket, the income in the lowest bracket is taxed at one rate and the remainder at the next rate. And if your taxable income puts you in the highest bracket, you pay tax at all six rates, with a different rate for each bracket. But unless your taxable income is more than $100,000, the point at which you must calculate the tax you owe, rather than look up the amount that's due in the tax tables the IRS provides, you may never be aware of paying at more than one rate.

FILING STATUS

Your **filing status** is the other factor that determines how much income tax you owe in any year. In fact, filing status is the major reason that people with similar incomes owe different amounts.

When you're supporting yourself—which means you get less than half of your support from someone else—you choose your filing status from among the five that are available, based on your actual living situation, or, more precisely, your situation as the IRS defines it.

- Single
- Married filing jointly
- Married filing separately
- Head of household
- Widow or widower with dependent child

When you do have a choice, such as filing joint or separate returns when you're married, you'll usually owe less tax if you do the conventional thing and file jointly. Plus, filing separately makes you ineligible for a number of tax-related benefits, like being able to convert a traditional IRA to a Roth IRA.

CHANGING THE RULES

Tax laws change all the time, but the basic structure has been in place since the 16th amendment to the US Constitution was adopted in 1913.

Often the changes are minimal, but the last major overhauls, in 2001 and 2003, introduced reduced tax rates, a plan to eliminate estate taxes, get rid of some inequities for married taxpayers, and expand the tax benefits you get for saving for education and retirement.

While these changes mean you may owe the government much less over the next decade than you would have if the law had not been passed, remember:

- Many of the provisions expire on December 31, 2010, or sooner, unless they're renewed
- The laws can always be changed again, before or after that date, increasing or decreasing what you owe

As a taxpayer, you have to stay alert so you can take the greatest advantage of the tax law provisions that can benefit you the most.

NOT THAT COMMON

There are some curiosities in the tax code that you may run up against from time to time. For example, if you live in the District of Columbia or one of the eleven states that recognizes common-law marriage, or if you lived in one of those states when you began your relationship, you can file a joint return with your partner even though you're not legally married. If you're interested, the eleven states are Alabama, Colorado, Iowa, Kansas, Montana, Oklahoma, Pennsylvania, Rhode Island, South Carolina, Texas, and Utah.

But if you live in the 39 other states, you can't file a joint return—even if you've been with the same person for years and met all the standards for a common-law marriage—one of which is filing a joint tax return.

Adjusting Your Income

Fortunately, you don't owe tax on every last nickel.

If you're looking for the bright side of paying income taxes, consider this: Your **taxable income**—the amount of income that's the base for calculating what you owe—is always less than your **total income**, sometimes called your gross income.

That's because the tax law—officially the Internal Revenue Code—lets you deduct certain amounts from your total income in figuring your taxable income. And you may even be able to subtract credits to reduce your actual tax.

WORKING THE NUMBERS

1 The process of finding the tax you owe begins with totaling your income. You add up all your earned and unearned income, including basic things like your salary, tips, interest, and bonuses. Your income may also include a list of things that might not occur to you, such as sick pay and unemployment. The IRS provides a fairly exhaustive list in the instructions that come with tax forms and in Publication 17, "Your Federal Income Tax."

2 The intermediary steps between your total income and your taxable income is finding your **adjusted gross income (AGI)** by subtracting your **adjustments**, or certain specific expenses listed on the tax form you use. (If you're eligible to use the 1040EZ, the process is a little different, but it's clearly spelled out on the form itself.)

Among the adjustments that will probably be relevant to you at this stage are interest on student loans, contributions to deductible IRAs or self-directed retirement plans, such as **Simplified Employee Pensions (SEPs)**, self-employment taxes, and alimony you pay.

SOME FREE LUNCH

A few—but not many—sources of income aren't taxed if you're on the receiving end, including gifts, tuition scholarships and some fellowships, tax-exempt interest from municipal bonds, and child support payments.

THE BOTTOM LINE AND BELOW

Once you know your taxable income, you look up the tax that's due on the tables the IRS provides, or, for taxable income over $100,000, calculate the amount

TAX TABLES

TAXING THE UNEARNED

Remember, you also owe tax on **unearned income** from your savings and investment accounts.

If you sell investments for more than you paid for them, you owe **capital gains tax** on your profit. Long-term gains on most assets you own for more than a year before you sell them are taxed at a lower rate than short-term gains or earned income. But they're still taxed.

If you're paid interest on a savings account, certificate of deposit (CD), or bond, you owe tax on that amount even if you leave the interest in your account to compound. The same is true for dividends you receive on stocks or mutual funds, whether or not you re-invest those earnings. The good news is that the tax on most dividends is figured at the long-term capital gains rate.

Banks, brokerage firms, mutual fund companies, and other financial institutions typically don't withhold income tax on the interest or dividends they pay you. So you have to estimate the income you anticipate each year. If it's substantial, you can either increase the amount you have withheld from your earned income or pay estimated taxes.

EXEMPTIONS DEDUCTIONS | STANDARD DEDUCTION | ITEMIZED DEDUCTION

3 Next, you subtract **exemptions** and **deductions** from your AGI to find your taxable income.

You get one exemption for yourself, two exemptions if you're married and filing a joint return, and one for each of your dependents. The exemption amount is indexed to inflation, so it changes a little bit each year.

One caution: If your income is above the limit the government sets, your eligibility to take personal exemptions decreases, resulting in a higher taxable income. In fact, if your income is high enough, you may not be able to take any exemptions at all.

If you're going to claim someone as a dependent and take an exemption, that person must qualify by meeting five tests, or standards, the IRS describes in the instructions provided with your tax return. People other than your children may pass the tests, but the rules are rather strict.

4 You can take either the **standard deduction**, an amount that covers certain personal expenses, or you can **itemize**, or list, your deductions and take that amount if it's higher than the standard. Most people don't bother itemizing, but if you have mortgage interest and real estate taxes, charitable contributions, or certain other expenses, itemizing may pay off in lower taxes.

But the only medical expenses you can deduct are amounts you paid yourself that are more than 7.5% of your AGI.

you owe. Everything you need is in the instructions that come with your form.

Next, you subtract any **credits** you qualify for. Credits are better than deductions or exemptions because they directly reduce the tax you owe, not your taxable income. But you have to qualify for them, usually by having spent money on things like education, foreign taxes, childcare or adoption expenses, or care for elderly or disabled dependents. Each credit requires that you attach an explanatory form to your tax return, and there are income and other restrictions that may limit your ability to claim some or all of them.

Finally, you compare what you owe with what you prepaid to see if you get a refund or have to write a check.

Keeping Records

When it comes to taxes, spring cleaning
takes on a whole new meaning.

Taxes seem to invite clutter. Tattered
shoeboxes and bulging envelopes stuffed
with hundreds of slips of paper are
staples of tax humor.

But there's a serious side to all
that mess. You need a year's worth of
financial documents to fill out your tax
return. And before one tax year ends,
the next tax year—with its own set of
essential records—has already started.

One way to avoid total confusion is
to keep all your records in one place. As
they arrive, or at least as often as once a
month, take the time to organize them by
category, date, or whatever works for you.

DOCUMENTING IT ALL

Certain documents are essential for
completing your tax return.

W-2 forms. If you're working
full- or part-time, you should get a
W-2 form from your employer no later
than the end of January. The form
reports what you earned for the year,
what was withheld for income taxes,
Social Security and Medicare, and any
additional deductions.

1099 forms. If you're a freelancer,
you'll get a 1099 from each job,
reporting the amount that you were
paid. If you're investing or saving, you'll
get a 1099 from each financial institution where you have an account. For
instance, you'll get a **1099-INT** to report
interest you earned and a **1099-DIV** to
report dividends on stocks and mutual
funds. Other 1099 forms report government payments, income from royalties
or rentals, and so forth.

The more you earn and the more
complicated your financial situation,
the more records you need. Here's
a potential list:

- Confirmations of purchase and sale
  prices of stocks and bonds that
  you sold
  during the
  year so you
  can figure
  your capi-
  tal gains
  (or losses)
- Statements
  of interest
  you paid
  on student
  loans, mort-
  gages, and
  investment accounts
- A statement confirming the contribution you made to a deductible IRA
- Records of uninsured medical and
  dental expenses that total more than
  7.5% of your adjusted gross income
- Records of state and local taxes
  you paid
- Records of expenses you paid for
  business travel or volunteer work for
  which you haven't been reimbursed

ENDLESS SLIPS OF PAPER

The IRS recommends holding onto
Copy C of your W-2 form until
you start receiving Social Security
benefits. That's so you can prove
what you've earned and where
you've worked if you think you're
not getting the right benefits.
That may be overkill, though.

Each year, several months before
your birthday, you get a statement
from the Social Security Administration reporting what's been credited
to your account. If you check each
year to be sure the new information
is accurate, and get it corrected if it
isn't, you shouldn't need to keep
50 years of W-2 forms.

Usually these records go back into your files after you've completed your tax form. But some experts suggest that if you have unusually large adjustments to income or itemized deductions that might trigger IRS questions, it can make sense to attach copies of your supporting documents.

HOLD ON!

So how long do you need to keep your tax return and the back-up documents after you file? In most cases, the IRS recommends at least three years. That's how long they have to **audit**, or examine, your return. But be sure to check your state's tax regulations, since some states have different audit rules.

You should keep your federal and state tax returns, as well as your W-2s, 1099s, and other important forms, in a safe place. In fact, if you've got a safe deposit box, you might want to store your actual returns there and keep copies at home.

There are a few tax-related documents you should hold onto indefinitely. For instance, if you've bought a home, you need to keep proof of what you paid for it and any money you spent on renovations. They can help reduce your capital gains if you ever sell. The same goes for any property you've inherited or received as a gift.

If you've sold any investments, you should keep proof of that sale for at least three years. And you should keep records of your contributions to tax-deferred and tax-exempt plans as long as there's a penny left in them.

In all other cases, just use your best judgment. If you think a receipt or check is relevant, then there's no harm in holding onto it for awhile.

SHEDDING THE EXCESS

If the need to be neat gets overpowering, there are documents you can get rid of.

When you get your W-2 from your employer, you can discard your paycheck stubs for the previous year. You also don't need to worry about keeping quarterly investment dividend or interest statements once you get the 1099 that reports them.

You don't need telephone bills, utility bills, or similar receipts for tax purposes, though you may want to hold onto them for a year to help track your living expenses and plan for the next year. And you do want to check each bill as it arrives to be sure your last payment was credited to your account before you discard the previous one.

Banks suggest you keep your account statements and cancelled checks (or photocopied versions of them) for several years. A good rule of thumb is, the longer the better.

HELPFUL HINT

To learn more about keeping tax records, look at IRS Publication 552, "Record-keeping for Individuals." You can get a copy in any IRS office, call 800-829-3676, order it online at www.irs.gov, or download a copy from that website.

Prepaying Taxes

You get a Hobson's choice with taxes: You can prepay or you can prepay.

Although the government insists you prepay what you owe in tax, the IRS generously provides two methods for doing it: withholding and estimating. Your problem is how to be sure you're paying the right amounts.

Withholding makes your life easier, even if you'd rather not have to share your earnings with Uncle Sam. The IRS doesn't set the amount that's withheld from your salary or wages. Your employer determines your withholding from the information you provide on **IRS Form W-4**. You fill out a W-4 whenever you begin a new job, and you can update an existing one at any time to increase or decrease the amount that's being taken out.

WITHHOLDING
By your employer

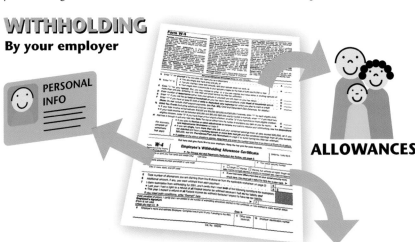

PERSONAL INFO

ALLOWANCES

FILING STATUS

DEALING WITH W-4
To complete the W-4, you must:
- Provide your name and Social Security number
- Indicate whether you're single, married, or married but withholding at the single rate
- Choose the number of **allowances** you claim, and decide whether you want an extra amount withheld

Sound easy? On the surface, it is. But there's a catch. What you're trying to do is to come as close as you can to matching the amount withheld with what you'll owe in taxes. That way you avoid the prospect of a penalty for underpaying and the pointlessness of overpaying.

Virtually the only wiggle room you have is in the number of allowances you claim—typically one for yourself, one for each dependent you can claim on your tax return, and one for each factor that reduces the tax you owe. The higher the number of allowances, the less will be withheld from your paycheck, and the higher your take-home pay will be. Conversely, claiming few or no allowances means your take-home pay will be lower but you'll prepay more.

If your tax situation is pretty simple—for example, if you have just one job and no investment income—you may be right on target by taking one allowance for yourself and one for each dependent. But if you discover in April, when you file your return, that way too much or too little has been withheld, you need to make some changes to your W-4.

HELP OR HINDRANCE?
To help you figure out the right number of allowances, the IRS provides a "Deductions and Adjustments Worksheet." It's about as difficult a document as you'll find anywhere. To use it, you need detailed information about your income, your expenses, your filing status, and any potential adjustments to income.

Don't hesitate to ask for help, either from your employer or a tax adviser. But be prepared to share last year's tax return

ESTIMATING
Quarterly payments

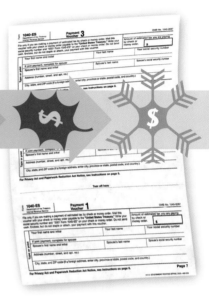

with the person who's helping you. And ask for an explanation of any solution that's suggested so you'll know how to tackle the problem the next time it comes up.

PAYING ESTIMATED TAXES

If you're self-employed or a freelancer, either full-time or in addition to working as an employee, the IRS expects you to estimate how much tax you'll owe for the year and pay part of it each quarter, in April, June, September, and January. You use Form 1040ES, "Estimated Tax for Individuals," to figure your estimated tax and make your payments.

The first payment is due for the first quarter in which you have taxable income. You can pay everything you expect to owe then, in a lump sum, or you can spread what you owe over the rest of the year. The usual way is to divide the total you're prepaying by four (or however many quarters are left) and pay it in equal amounts. That's fine if your income is fairly regular and predictable. But you may have a problem if it's not—something that's fairly common when you work for yourself.

The solution may be to recalculate the tax you owe each quarter to find the minimum due on each of the remaining dates. You can get IRS Publication 505, "Tax Withholding and Estimated Tax," or you can consult a tax adviser. In fact, you may want to find one who specializes in clients with self-employment income.

DOUBLE IDENTITY

If you're paying estimated income taxes, perhaps because you're a freelancer or self-employed, you have to pay Social Security and Medicare taxes, called **self-employment taxes**, yourself. The Social Security that's due is 12.4% of your earnings up to the annual cap, which increases every year to reflect inflation increases. You must also pay 2.9% of your total earnings for Medicare, with no cap.

Those are twice the percentages that your employer withholds if you have a job. That's because you're paying two shares—yours as employee and yours as employer. The consolation is that you can deduct half the total, equal to the employer's share, as an adjustment to income on your tax return. That reduces your AGI, and your taxable income.

Filing Your Return

There's a when, what, and how of taxes: when to file, what to file, and how to file.

Paying taxes is no fun, and sometimes it seems like filing the forms themselves is just as bad. But if not having to file a tax return sounds appealing, think again.

The only times you don't have to file are:
- When your income is so low it falls below the limit set by Congress for your filing status
- If you're being claimed as a dependent, earn even less than the already low floor for non-dependents, and have only a small amount of unearned income

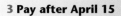

1 File and pay by April 15

2 Pay by April 15, and get a four-month filing extension

3 Pay after April 15

4 Pay as much as possible on April 15, and the rest in installments

5 File after August 15

WATCHING THE CLOCK

Although the official date for filing your return and paying any outstanding tax you owe is April 15, you've actually got several options:

1 **File and pay by April 15.** You won't face penalties or have to make interest payments.

2 **Pay by April 15, and get a four-month filing extension.** You can get a filing extension until August 15 if you submit Form 4868 by April 15. But you still have to pay your taxes by April 15—usually at least 90% of what you owe—and you'll be charged interest and penalties if you don't pay on time.

3 **Pay after April 15.** With or without an official filing extension, you'll rack up penalties and interest until you pay all of what you owe.

4 **Pay as much as possible on April 15, and the rest in installments.** You can submit Form 9465, which is a request for an installment payment plan, with your return. The IRS will notify you within 30 days if your request is approved. If it is, you can pay the rest of what you owe in installments. You'll also have to pay a penalty, interest, and a one-time processing fee.

CHOOSING THE RIGHT FORM

In most cases, the less complicated your financial life, the easier it will be to prepare your tax return.

The IRS provides three forms, the nine-question **1040EZ**, the slightly more complicated **1040A**, and the detailed **1040**. You can use the simplest one you qualify for, based on your income, where that money comes from, and whether you're claiming dependents, deductions, credits, capital gains, or other adjustments.

ELIGIBILITY RULES

You're eligible to use the 1040EZ if the following apply to you:
- Taxable income under $100,000
- Single, or married and filing jointly with your spouse
- Not claiming any dependents
- Under age 65
- Earned income only from wages, tips, taxable scholarships and fellowships, or unemployment compensation
- No itemized deductions, adjustments, or tax credits other than the earned income credit

5 **File after August 15.** If you've requested a four-month extension but still need more time to file, the IRS might give you an extra two-month extension, to October 15. You'll need to submit Form 2688, along with an explanation of why you need the extension. Apply early, because if you don't get approved you'll still need to file by August 15.

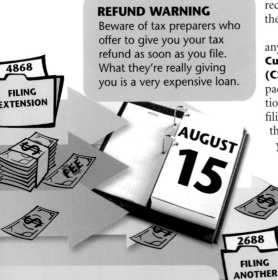

REFUND WARNING
Beware of tax preparers who offer to give you your tax refund as soon as you file. What they're really giving you is a very expensive loan.

You're eligible to use the 1040A if the following apply to you:
- Taxable income under $100,000
- No itemized deductions or adjustments, except for IRA contributions or student loan interest
- No self-employment, capital gains, or rental income
- Eligible to claim dependent care, as well as several credits, including credits for the elderly and disabled, child, education, earned income, and adoption

You're required to use the 1040 if any of the following apply to you:
- Taxable income above $100,000
- Self-employment income
- Capital gains or losses from investments
- Itemized deductions
- Receive or pay alimony

After you've filed a return for the first time, the IRS will automatically send you the same form for the next tax year—or a simpler one if you qualify to use it.

HOW TO FILE

In the past, you had to file your return by mail, making sure it was postmarked by midnight on April 15—or April 16 or 17 if the 15th fell on Saturday or Sunday. You can still do it that way. But the IRS has kept up with the times, and you have other options.

Telefiling. If you qualify to file the 1040EZ, you may be able to do it over the phone. But you've got to receive a Telefile package from the IRS.

You can call Telefile at any time. All you need is the **Customer Service Number (CSN)** included in the Telefile package and the basic information about your income and filing status. A computer does the math, and tells you whether you have a balance due or a refund coming. You'll also get a confirmation number, which you should hold onto as proof that you've completed your return.

Electronic Filing. Whatever form you qualify to use, you can file electronically—completely paperlessly if you choose—either on your own or using a tax preparer. In fact, in most states you can file your federal and state income taxes at the same time.

All you need to handle the filing yourself is access to a computer and tax software approved by the IRS, which you can buy, download from the Internet, or use online. You can get a list of approved software or sites at the IRS website, www.irs.gov. Just click on the e-file button.

Whichever electronic method you use, you can expect a faster refund (if you have one coming) than if you'd filed the conventional way. For an even faster turnaround, you can have the refund direct deposited in your bank or credit union account.

If you owe money, you can pay by credit card or debit card. But remember, there is a fee for using a credit card. And if you don't pay the full amount of your bill by the date it's due, you'll owe a finance charge to the issuer.

Worse still, if you have an unpaid balance on your card when you charge your taxes, you may owe a finance charge on your total tax bill from the day you authorize the payment.

www.irs.gov

Getting Help

If you're a tax rookie, you can team up with the pros.

There's something about the prospect of filling out a tax return that most people find intimidating. But don't despair. You can get the help you need.

The Internal Revenue Service (IRS) is the place to start. You can visit its website at www.irs.gov, stop by an IRS office, or call one of its toll-free phone numbers.

You can get line-by-line guidance for doing your return in comprehensive guides from J.K. Lasser, Ernst & Young, Consumer Reports, and others. These books are cheap, they're updated every year, and they provide some handy tax-saving tips. Many of them are based on IRS Publication 17, "Your Federal Income Taxes," which you can get free from the IRS or download to your computer.

What might be even more appealing is some of the tax preparation software, available on CD or online, that walks you step-by-step through the filing process. You can find a list of approved software on the IRS website by clicking on the e-file button and then on the list of partners. There are also a number of financial websites that offer free advice and general guidance.

IN PERSON

You may want to get some help from the person who has been doing your return—perhaps one of your parents or a tax-savvy friend or relative—or from a tax professional. In fact, almost half of all taxpayers pay someone else to do their taxes.

Finding the right person for the job can be almost as daunting as the prospect of doing your taxes yourself, in part because there are so many people advertising tax preparation services, and in part because it can be hard to evaluate a preparer's expertise. Often a recommendation from family, friends, or coworkers is the best way to start your search.

Unfortunately, there's no qualifying test or licensing system required for people calling themselves tax preparers, though many of them provide excellent help at modest fees. Some preparers work independently, while others work for nationwide commercial tax preparation services.

If your tax situation is complicated because you have income from a number of sources, major tax-deductible expenses, or business expenses, you may want to move up the financial adviser ladder to work with an **enrolled agent** or a **certified public accountant (CPA)**.

I tried to use tax software to do my taxes but had more than one job in the tax year. One job had a 401(k) and one didn't. The program wouldn't complete my return unless I entered 401(k) information for each job. I ended up getting my taxes prepared... I had to pay 50 bucks to an accountant.
— Frantz A., 23

Enrolled agents have either worked for the IRS or passed a comprehensive IRS-sponsored exam. CPAs must pass rigorous state qualifying exams. And both must meet continuing education requirements, which helps ensure they'll be up-to-date on changing tax laws—something that may be an issue for most of the current decade.

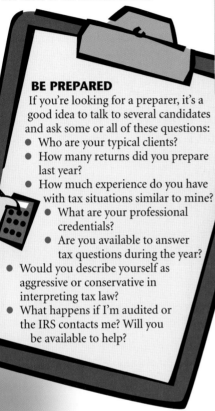

BE PREPARED

If you're looking for a preparer, it's a good idea to talk to several candidates and ask some or all of these questions:

- Who are your typical clients?
- How many returns did you prepare last year?
- How much experience do you have with tax situations similar to mine?
  - What are your professional credentials?
  - Are you available to answer tax questions during the year?
- Would you describe yourself as aggressive or conservative in interpreting tax law?
- What happens if I'm audited or the IRS contacts me? Will you be available to help?

WHAT HELP COSTS

Surprisingly, tax help won't break the bank. Most of the standard guides cost less than $20, and computer software programs are rarely more than $30.

If you use a commercial preparer for a fairly basic form, you can expect to pay up to $75, depending on whom you use. For a more complicated return, an enrolled agent may charge between $100 and $300, and a CPA up to $500.

And do your homework. For example, you should have a sense of which form you qualify to use. If a potential preparer insists you use the 1040 when you know you can use the 1040A, that may be a sign to look for someone different.

Remember, too, that being comfortable with the person you'll be working with is also important. For example, you may prefer a conservative, play-it-safe approach to deductions over an aggressive one. And at the end of the day, you're responsible for the accuracy of your return, no matter who prepares it.

A WORD TO THE WISE

Help from IRS publications and Web resources is free and accurate, and always a good starting place. Assistance from an IRS representative is free as well. But experts suggest that you get a written copy of the advice you get from an IRS representative. Otherwise the agency isn't responsible if you use incorrect information to report your income or calculate the tax you owe. If fines or interest payments are due, they'll be your responsibility.

WHAT CAN GO WRONG

If you file your return on time, pay what's due, and don't play fast and loose with the rules, you probably won't be hearing from the IRS. But you can make mistakes that the agency's software catches. Then you'll get a notice called a CP-2000, with the likely result that you'll owe additional tax, and perhaps interest and penalties. You can pay up or you can respond with an explanation.

Sometimes a phone conversation will handle the problem, though you should always send a written confirmation that spells out how the inquiry was resolved, keeping a copy in your files. If the problem is more complex, you may want to get professional tax or legal advice. When you have to send documents, send copies, not originals. And keep a file of the entire exchange.

If there are bigger problems, you may face an examination, or **audit**. Then you have to show the IRS that all the information you provided on your form is correct. If you can't back up your claims, you're likely to get a bill for what the IRS thinks you owe, plus penalties and interest.

AUDIT!

Taxing Matters

You may end up knowing more about taxes than you thought there was to know.

GET SOME EXCISE

Did you ever wonder about the extra taxes you pay when you buy a gallon of gas or an airline ticket, or the ones that get tacked on to your phone bill? The federal government imposes **excise taxes** on the manufacture, sale, or consumption of specific goods and services produced and used within the country. In addition, state and local governments often add excise taxes of their own.

Price
+ Excise tax
= Retail price
+ State tax
= What you pay

Instead of being levied as a percentage of the price, as sales taxes are, excise taxes are figured as a per-unit cost—such as the federal charge of 18.3 cents on a gallon of gas. The best-known, and oldest, excise taxes increase the prices of tobacco and alcohol, as well as crude oil and fuels.

In fact, high excise taxes, not the wholesale price of gas, help explain why you pay more to fill your fuel tank in some states than you do in others.

As prevalent as excise taxes seem, the revenue they produce amounts to less than 10% of all the tax the federal government collects. Some of the money ends up in special trust funds that are used to improve highways or airports, or to clean up hazardous chemical spills. Part of the excise tax on phone bills is designated to pay for Internet access in public schools.

BACKUP WITHHOLDING

If you receive income that's reported on a Form 1099—as dividends and interest are, for example—you'll be asked to provide your Social Security number, also called your Tax Identification Number or TIN, and sign Form W-9

WHAT'S AN AUDIT?

If the IRS thinks you owe more tax than you paid, the agency schedules an **audit**, or an examination of your tax return and the records that back up your claims. They're checking to see if you've reported all your income and are entitled to all the adjustments and deductions you've claimed.

There are actually several types of audits. A **correspondence audit** is conducted by mail. You supply copies of the specific records that the IRS requests, and you get a letter reporting the agency's conclusions—usually with a bill for additional tax.

An **office audit** takes place in an IRS office. You're told ahead of time what the questions are and which records to bring with you to review with a tax auditor.

A **field audit** takes place in your home, your office, or the office of a tax professional who can represent you before the IRS. It's conducted by a revenue agent, who can examine your entire return and all your supporting documents.

ADDED VALUE?

A **Value-Added Tax (VAT)** is a national sales tax widely used in Europe, Canada, Mexico, and other countries either to supplement or replace a national income tax. Like other sales taxes, a VAT is a flat tax. But it's imposed on sales at each stage in the production of something of value, from the sale of raw materials to retail distribution.

VAT due on **PRODUCTION**   VAT due on **WHOLESALE**   VAT due on **RETAIL**

which certifies that you're not subject to **backup withholding**. That means you don't have to have tax withheld on this type of income, but only pay the tax owed when you file your return.

If the IRS hasn't notified you that you must pay backup withholding, which could happen if they suspect you are underreporting interest or dividend income, you can sign with a clear conscience. If you don't complete the form, income taxes will be withheld. A 28% withholding rate applies through December 2010.

It's possible you may prevail and owe nothing more. And if you disagree with the IRS finding that additional tax is due, you can appeal. You can even take your case to court if you can't reach a compromise solution, but it's a slow and expensive process.

CORRESPONDENCE AUDIT

OFFICE AUDIT

FIELD AUDIT

For example, when you pay VAT on a new wool jacket, yours is the last in a series of VAT payments that started with the sale of the wool, moved on through the production of the cloth, the manufacture of the jacket, the purchase by the wholesaler, and the order from the retail shop.

Is a VAT possible in the US? One of the factors that works against enacting it is that a national sales tax would probably restrict what states could collect in sales taxes of their own. And sales taxes are a primary source of state revenue.

TAXPAYER BILL OF RIGHTS

IRS Publication 1, "Your Rights as a Taxpayer," is sometimes described as a taxpayer's bill of rights.

Among the things you're guaranteed are the rights to:

- Know why you're being asked for information, how it will be used, and what will happen if you don't provide it
- Produce only the documents the IRS asks for
- Bring someone with you to any meetings with the IRS and record any meetings with an IRS representative
- Interrupt any meeting with the IRS if you need professional advice
- Be represented by someone authorized to practice before the IRS, such as an attorney, certified public accountant, or enrolled agent
- Propose installment payments for taxes that are due

DOING THE WASH

Did you know that federal law requires banks and businesses to report deposits and payments of more than $10,000 when they're made in cash?

It's one of the tools the government uses to try to prevent **money laundering**, or schemes to route illegally acquired cash through legitimate bank accounts and businesses to make the money appear as if it had been earned legitimately.

INDEX